PROPHETIC ACTIVATION

PROPHETIC ACTIVATION

JOHN ECKHARDT

CHARISMA
HOUSE

Most CHARISMA HOUSE BOOK GROUP products are available at special quantity discounts for bulk purchase for sales promotions, premiums, fund-raising, and educational needs. For details, write Charisma House Book Group, 600 Rinehart Road, Lake Mary, Florida 32746, or telephone (407) 333-0600.

PROPHETIC ACTIVATION by John Eckhardt
Published by Charisma House
Charisma Media/Charisma House Book Group
600 Rinehart Road
Lake Mary, Florida 32746
www.charismahouse.com

Unless otherwise noted, all Scripture quotations are taken from the Modern English Version. Copyright © 2014 by Military Bible Association. Used by permission. All rights reserved.

Scripture quotations marked AMPC are taken from the Amplified® Bible, Copyright © 1954, 1958, 1962, 1964, 1965, 1987 by The Lockman Foundation. Used by permission. (www.Lockman.org).

Scripture quotations marked CEB are from the Common English Bible. Copyright © 2011 Common English Bible. Used by permission.

Cover design by Justin Evans

Visit the author's website at
www.johneckhardtministries.com.

Library of Congress Cataloging-in-Publication Data:
Names: Eckhardt, John, 1957- author.
Title: Prophetic activation / John Eckhardt.
Description: Lake Mary, Florida : Charisma House, 2016.
Identifiers: LCCN 2016008941| ISBN 9781629987095 (paperback) | ISBN
   9781629987552 (e-book)
Subjects: LCSH: Gifts, Spiritual. | Prophecies. | BISAC: RELIGION / Christian
   Life / Spiritual Growth.
Classification: LCC BT767.3 .E26 2016 | DDC 234/.13--dc23
LC record available at http://lccn.loc.gov/2016008941

16 17 18 19 20 21— 10 9 8 7 6 5 4 3
Printed in the United States of America

CONTENTS

CHAPTER 3:   ACTIVATIONS PROMPTED
BY THE NAMES OF GOD............ 35

CHAPTER 4:   ACTIVATIONS PROMPTED
BY SPIRITUAL VIRTUES 41

CHAPTER 7: PROPHETIC PRAYER
ACTIVATIONS 58

CHAPTER 8: PROPHETIC SONGS AND
WORSHIP ACTIVATIONS 63

CHAPTER 12: CORPORATE MINISTRY ACTIVATIONS 90

BE RELEASED INTO A GREATER PROPHETIC DIMENSION

O UR GOD SPEAKS! This is what separates Him from the idols men have worshipped throughout time and around the world. Idols are dumb (cannot speak). Some are fashioned—carved, molded, or shaped—with mouths, but they do not speak. Our God sees! Many idols have eyes, but they do not see. They are inanimate and their form has been designed by the imaginations of men.

> Their idols are silver and gold, the work of men's hands. They have mouths, but they cannot speak; eyes, but they cannot see; they have ears, but they cannot hear.
>
> —PSALM 115:4–5

> What profit is a carved image when its maker has carved it, a cast image, and a teacher of lies, that its maker trusts in what he has shaped when he makes mute idols?
>
> —HABAKKUK 2:18

> You know that you were Gentiles, carried away to these dumb idols, however you were led.
>
> —1 CORINTHIANS 12:2

Our God is the living God who moves throughout the spiritual and physical realms in all power and authority as the Creator of every living thing. He desires to commune with His creation. One way He does this is through prophecy, which includes hearing, speaking, and seeing what God is saying. God speaks to and through His people to share with us His many wonderful works and to declare His thoughts toward us. As Psalm 40:5 says, "O LORD my God, You have done many wonderful works, and Your thoughts toward us cannot be compared; if I would declare and speak of them, they are more than can be numbered." Through the power of His Spirit we are given the ability to not only hear God, but also to see what He is doing. *Prophetic Activation* is designed to kick-start and develop believers in all these areas.

WHAT IS PROPHETIC ACTIVATION AND ITS BENEFITS?

Let me say this...you can begin now to start activating the prophetic streams from within your belly, coming out of dormancy, into the front line of what God is doing in the earth today. You can move from pathetic to prophetic and declare a new sound in this generation. But it starts within your belly and mouth.[1]

—TIM AND THERESA EARLY

To activate something is to start it off, trigger it, or set it in motion. Prophetic activations are spiritual exercises that use words, actions, phrases, objects, Scripture verses, worship songs and dance, prophetic prayers, and more to trigger the prophetic gifts and help believers in every area of life and ministry to flow freely as they are commissioned to release God's word in the earth. They set in motion prophetic utterances, songs, and movement that will bring great blessing to the members of local churches and ministries and the world.

Activations are designed to break down the barriers of fear, doubt, timidity, and ignorance that hinder and prevent people from operating in prophecy. They will also provide people an opportunity to minster, some for the first time, in a safe and loving environment.

Activations rekindle and fan the flame of ministries that have become stagnant in the prophetic flow. We all need times of rekindling and reignition. Prophetic activations will reignite believers and churches to prophesy. Motionless churches need to be set in motion. Prophetic activations can get us moving again.

> That is why I would remind you to stir up (rekindle the embers of, fan the flame of, and keep burning) the [gracious] gift of God, [the inner fire] that is in you by means of the laying on of my hands [with those of the elders at your ordination].
>
> —2 TIMOTHY 1:6, AMPC

I was exposed to prophetic activations in 1989 through the ministry of Drs. Buddy and Mary Crum of Life Center Ministries. I invited them to our church. They came and activated, trained, confirmed, and launched us in prophetic gifts and ministry. Since then I have seen the growth of our prophetic groups and teams over the years. However, there have been times when we have become stagnant, and we have had to break through into another level. But we knew how to use the activations to stir up our gifts and bring revival when needed.

Now I travel all over the world—sometimes alone or with my prophetic team—activating believers in prophetic ministry. Some of those who are in prophetic ministry at my church have become so strong in the prophetic anointing that they have launched their own international ministries. They too travel the world preaching and teaching, and activating and releasing prophets among the nations. God is always challenging us to come higher and expand more.

There are many creative ways to activate believers. I have placed over one hundred of them, organized in categories, throughout the chapters in this book. Activations should be simple and fun. Saints should enjoy moving in the things of the Spirit. People of all ages can be involved. Activations will bring a new excitement to any church, and they also can be a catalyst for revival and glory.

The value of different activations is that they will break your limitations and give you the ability to operate in different ways. Don't be limited to your favorite way, but move in different ways and administrations. The prophetic anointing must never become boring and routine but should always be exciting and new. God has many surprises for us, and the prophetic anointing will always release new things.

With the diversity of gifts present in the body of Christ, activations are important because we want to see people operate correctly and accurately in their unique prophetic anointing. We don't want to release people who could potentially do damage and harm to others. We need training, and sometimes correction, in operating in prophecy. Activations provide a safe environment to help people learn how to operate in excellence in this important area. Although prophecy comes from God, it is released through human vessels, and therefore it can be tainted and sometimes delivered inaccurately. As 2 Corinthians 4:7 says, "We have this treasure in earthen vessels."

Prophetic activations are not designed to make everyone a prophet—only God can call and commission a prophet. Activations are simply designed to stir people to grow in whatever level they are called to. There may be people participating and leading activations who are prophets, some with the gift of prophecy, and some who have the spirit of prophecy as a result of being filled with the Holy Ghost, but there also may be people who are psalmists, minstrels, intercessors, counselors, preachers, teachers, and dancers in the activations. Activations will stir them and cause them all to move more in faith and inspiration.

Prophetic activations will also raise the prophetic level in a church, region, or territory. This level is measured by how many mature prophets are ministering in a region, how many believers are operating prophetically in a region, how many churches are operating in prophetic ministry in a region, and the level of prophetic intercession and worship in a region.

The Prophet Samuel is an example of how one person can influence a region. When Samuel was born, there was no prophetic activity in the nation (1 Sam. 3:1). By the time Samuel anointed Saul, there were companies of prophets ministering (1 Sam. 10). In 1 Samuel 19 we find Samuel at Naioth in Ramah standing over the prophets. The prophetic atmosphere was so strong that everyone who came into this atmosphere began to prophesy.

Samuel was responsible for developing emerging prophets in Israel. The Bible does not give us the details of this training. There probably was musical and scriptural training involved, and possibly impartation from Samuel into the lives of the prophets. Samuel brought prophetic ministry to a new level in Israel, which outlived him and continued in generations to come. This is what I intend to do by releasing to you these activations that have been so instrumental in my personal walk with Christ as well as in the life of my church.

WHO SHOULD FACILITATE AND PARTICIPATE IN PROPHETIC ACTIVATION?

Leaders who have a desire to see the local church and the people released into a greater prophetic dimension should employ the strategy of prophetic activations. We cannot teach people how to prophesy, but we can help them hear the voice of God and speak the words they hear with faith and confidence. Prophetic activations should be done in a loving environment where people feel comfortable. There is no better place to be than being around loving leaders and believers who have no motive other than to bless and encourage.

If you are a leader of a ministry, small group, or

church, set aside some time to do activations. If you are a member at a church that operates in the prophetic anointing, bring up this idea to your pastor. If you attend a church that is not open to prophetic ministry, connect with a group of mature prophets and have them confirm and activate you. When you participate in prophetic activations, you will see a new momentum in your prophetic flow.

Paul admonishes the church to "desire spiritual gifts" (1 Cor. 14:1) and "covet to prophesy" (1 Cor. 14:39, kjv). Those who desire this important administration of the Holy Spirit should take the time to be a part of a prophetic activation. Activation will stir believers and help them move into a strong prophetic flow. Even those who have experience in the prophetic anointing can benefit from activations. Sometimes people need to be restored and rekindled. We can become dormant in our gifts. We need to continually stir up these gifts.

> While every Spirit-filled believer can prophecy [*sic*] as a general grace God gave to the entire Church (Joel 2:28–29; Acts 2:15–18; 1 Cor. 14:31), the measure we experience the prophetic and are able to walk in it is determined by our hunger. If we can live without it, we most likely will.[2]
>
> —Benjamin Schäfer

Those who desire to prophesy should understand the great benefits of prophecy. Prophecy can encourage, comfort, build up, confirm, strengthen, impart, release, renew, refresh, heal, deliver, illuminate, enlighten, direct, expose, warn, convict, correct, bless, quicken, and restore. These many benefits alone should cause every leader, church, and believer to desire to prophesy. I have personally seen lives transformed and changed in over eighty nations through the power of prophecy.

But prophets and prophetic people should do more than just prophesy. They should also train and teach others in this area. Every believer should be able to hear the voice of God and release a word on a consistent basis. The prophetic dimension will also affect every area of the church, including the praise and worship, prayer, preaching, teaching, counseling, evangelism, and the arts. Prophetic churches will be a blessing to their cities, nations, and communities because they release the word of the Lord and reveal the heart of God.

IN WHAT ENVIRONMENT SHOULD PROPHETIC ACTIVATIONS BE CARRIED OUT?

Prophetic activations can be done in small or large groups. Groups can consist of believers who are on different levels of the prophetic anointing. There are people who are advanced or intermediate, and some may be beginners. It is good to have a mixture of people on different levels to sharpen and strengthen one another during the activations.

Some people will have a stronger prophetic flow, depending on their level of faith and their knowledge of the Word. But everyone can receive an impartation during a prophetic activation and become stronger in the prophetic flow.

We should follow after love and desire spiritual gifts, but we should especially desire to prophesy (1 Cor. 14:1). Not only should we desire to prophesy, but also we should desire to excel in it. First Corinthians 14:12 reads, "So, seeing that you are zealous of spiritual gifts, seek that you may *excel* to the edifying of the church" (emphasis added). Activations are designed for believers who not only have a desire to prophesy but also want to excel in this area. *Excel* means to be exceptionally good at or proficient in an activity or subject. Prophetic people should minister in excellence. Prophetic activations are designed to help believers develop and minister with excellence and accuracy.

Prophetic activations are designed to help believers sharpen one another in the area of prophecy. Proverbs 27:17 reads, "As one piece of iron sharpens another…" (ERV). *Sharpen* means to improve or cause to improve. There are times we need to sharpen the ax. Sometimes we can become dull in our gifting, and we need to sharpen ourselves. Ecclesiastes 10:10 reads, "If you don't sharpen your ax, it will be harder to use" (CEV).

In prophetic activations we generally place the parameters of the prophetic word to include edification, exhortation, and comfort (1 Cor. 14:3). This provides an atmosphere of safety for people who are opening themselves up to receive a word.

By doing this we are limiting the chance of error and affecting a person in a negative way. We don't want people hearing words about "premature death" or "whom to marry."

We don't want them to hear disturbing things such as, "I see a dark cloud following you," "Witches are after you," and so on. Although these kinds of words are possible, we leave them to more experienced prophets in a different setting.

Prophetic activations provide a safe environment for people to be stirred and activated in the area of prophecy. Prophecy does not replace prayer, preaching, teaching, praise, worship, and other areas that give a believer a balanced lifestyle. Prophetic activations are necessary because the prophetic area has often been underdeveloped, while the other aspects of the Christian life have been more developed.

During an activation, it is important for the people to follow instructions. This is not the place for rebellious and spooky people to try to hijack the prophetic flow and show off their gifts. Submission to godly authority should be a core value of the prophetic ministry, and rebellion is as the sin of witchcraft.

> Prophetic activation exercises are meant to equip with practical tools for hearing the voice of God. Eventually you will be able to utilize those tools in every sort of situations: during ministry time at your local church, in everyday life conversations with others, while writing emails or simply praying for others in your private time with the Lord. They will help you flow in the prophetic in your everyday life.[3]
>
> —BENJAMIN SCHÄFER

When participating in the activation exercises, we should give only what we receive regardless if it makes sense or not. Don't worry if you receive something from the Lord that does not make sense to you. You would be surprised to learn that what does not make sense to you may be life changing to the person to whom you are ministering.

Geoff and Gina Poulter of Rhema Outreach Ministries encourage those moving into prophetic ministry to not despise the day of small beginnings. Everyone has to start somewhere.

> When we are running a "Prophecy School" or workshop on prophecy we find that most attendees are able to operate in this gift at a basic level—the challenge then is for them to develop the gift. None of us starts off as mature in any of the gifts of the Holy Spirit and prophecy is no different. God is a loving Father and knows that we need to grow in both faith and understanding.[4]

Always remember that the Bible, as the perfect revelation of Jesus and the infallible Word of God, is the absolute standard for weighing and assessing all revelation (2 Tim. 3:16; Col. 2:18–19; John 1:14).

> Prophecy is not just about communicating God's mind, but also His heart.[5]

—STEVE THOMPSON

WHAT TO DO IF YOUR CHURCH DOES NOT HAVE
PROPHETIC MINISTRY OR TRAINING

Prophecy has been despised before. Moses, finally convinced that God wanted to delegate his governing authority to a larger number, called seventy elders to a "committee meeting" at the tabernacle. Two failed to show up. The Spirit of God fell on the sixty-eight who attended. But the Spirit also came upon the two who remained in the camp who began to prophesy as well. Every one wanted them to stop, uncomfortable at the direct voice of God and jealous for Moses' uniqueness as God's prophet. They reported the incident to Moses and demanded that he stop them. One can almost see Moses chuckling, and then longingly reflecting on the blessedness of the Spirit's presence in his life: "Would that all the Lord's people were prophets, that the Lord would put his Spirit upon them!" (Numbers 11:29).[6]

—DR. RALPH F. WILSON

I have been asked many times, as I have participated in prophetic roundtables around the country, what to do if a church is not active in prophetic ministry. Some have wondered if they should just start their own church or move to a different church because the church they attend does not operate in the prophetic anointing. Unless you have a grace to start a church, I wouldn't recommend that you do that. Starting churches is really an apostolic function, although prophets can start churches. I don't recommend that you become a fringe group away from the local church where you meet only outside the church. Instead get a core group of people together who are also interested in the prophetic gift and pray and study together. Read books on the subject. Come together and discuss them. Use the group to stay sharpened, connected, and inspired so that you won't dry up and die spiritually.

I also recommend that you become activated. You can attend a prophetic conference to receive activation. Then connect with a prophetic association or network so you can consistently stay in contact with mature prophetic people. ElijahList.com/links has a listing of prophetic ministries you can access. But you still need to be submitted to a local church as well, to be able to hear the Word. Also consider connecting with the authors of the books you are reading to receive activation and impartation.

If your church doesn't flow prophetically but is a fellowship that preaches and teaches the Word, has good worship, and is filled with love, it is important that you remain connected and accountable. You don't want to be a renegade prophet who is not connected or accountable to anybody—not submitted to any authority. Prophets who are all alone and don't listen to anyone are sometimes walking in rebellion. They are proud and independent. This is when a prophetic person can really get into trouble, because if he is off on his own and is operating in error, no one can correct him.

Being a part of a prophetic team, a prophetic company, or a prophetic church will bring you into accountability with other prophets. In 1 Corinthians 14:29–30 it says,

"Let the prophets speak, two or three, and let the others judge." Prophets can judge one another because prophets know prophets. They can tell when a prophet is wrong or when he is bitter, rebellious, independent, getting into false doctrine, or becoming controlling.

I know prophets can be persecuted and rejected, but if someone is always saying, "Nobody loves me. I am persecuted. Nobody trusts me," it could be that they are just rebellious and won't submit to anybody. I am very wary of people who have no friends, no relationships, no accountability, no local church, and never submit. They just want to pop up and prophesy.

This goes against God's instruction that prophets are to be *a part of the church*. "God has put these in the church…prophets…" (1 Cor. 12:28). Remember that under the old covenant prophets were primarily often isolated and alone because they were dealing with an apostate nation. Now under the new covenant the church is different. The church is a place full of people who are born again, new creatures, and who are also filled with the Spirit of God. A prophet can never say, "I'm outside the church." Even though you can't be in certain churches because they don't accept it or they fight it, I understand that. But the prophet is supposed to be part of the church, functioning inside the church. The prophet is a part of the body. Your hand does not run off and say, "I'm not part of the body anymore."

I am a pastor. I am a shepherd. I believe in the local church. I love the local church, and even though the local church can vex me, I never separate myself from the local church. Even as an apostle, I am accountable to other leaders, and I am accountable to my elders. I don't say, "I am the apostle. You don't tell me anything." No. If I get off course and if my lifestyle is not right, they have a right to correct me and challenge me.

So it is very important that you remain connected to a good Bible-believing fellowship, where the Word of God is honored and taught. If there is no openness to the prophetic gift, get with other prophetic believers and pray and study together, as I have already stated. Join a network of prophets. Buy prophetic books. Attend prophetic conferences. Buy CDs, listen to podcasts, and follow strong prophetic leaders in social media so that you continue to stir and strengthen your gift. Then pray and believe God to raise the prophetic level in your region. Remember, even as Elijah thought he was the only one, God reminded him, "I have preserved seven thousand in Israel" (1 Kings 19:18). Sometimes you think you are the only one, but there is always a remnant moving with God.

See more of my thoughts on this in my book *God Still Speaks.* In chapter 4 there is a section titled "Anointing flows from the head down." Refer to it for proper order if you are not a leader in the church but have a desire for prophetic ministry. You must have the proper authority in a church body to enact change in the vision of the church.

PLACES WHERE PROPHETS GROW AND FLOURISH

Prophetic activation allows you to be among those who prophesy. Being around those who prophesy can pull you into the prophetic flow. This is what happened to Saul. The Prophet Samuel said to Saul, "...you will meet a group of prophets coming down from the high place with a harp, a tambourine, a flute, and a lyre before them. And they will prophesy. And the Spirit of the LORD will come upon you, and you will prophesy with them. And you will be turned into another man" (1 Sam. 10:5–6).

There are certain places and atmospheres that cause prophets to grow and flourish. I listed these in chapter 1 of my book *Prophet, Arise!* They are here as a reminder so that you can see what places are geared toward prophetic activation, training, equipping, impartation, and confirmation. This list will also give you ideas on where you can go to grow in your gift, what groups you may be able to join or start, if you are part of a church that does not flow prophetically.

Prophetic families

God can raise up your children to be prophets. God called Jeremiah when he was a child. Prophetic children must be handled differently; they are not like other children. They are unique and very sensitive to the Spirit of God and the spirit realm.

I raised up some of your sons as prophets, and some of your young men as Nazirites. Is it not so, O children of Israel? says the LORD.

—AMOS 2:11

But the LORD said to me, "Do not say, 'I am a youth.' For you shall go everywhere that I send you, and whatever I command you, you shall speak."

—JEREMIAH 1:7

Prophetic communities: a company of prophets

When they came to the hill, a group of prophets met him. And the Spirit of God came upon him, and he prophesied among them.

—1 SAMUEL 10:10

[First Samuel 10:10] is the first mention of "a company (cord, chain, or band) of prophets" (Nabhis). There were previously individual prophets. And on one occasion the seventy elders prophesied (Numbers 11:25), and Moses said, "Would God that all the Lord's people were prophets, and that the Lord would put his Spirit upon them." But until the time of Samuel there was no association or community, college or school, of prophets. [The prophet Samuel's] language shows his intimate relation to this "company," of which he was doubtless the founder....Its formation was due to a newly awakened religious life among the people, and intended as a means of deepening and extending it.[7]

This community of prophets was also active at the time of Elijah and Elisha. These companies consisted of women as well, such as Huldah, who is called a prophetess in 2 Kings 22:14.

These prophets came together in community to encourage each other and build up their gifts. They worshipped together, ate together, and sometimes lived together. The strength of their gifts did not develop in a vacuum. They were nurtured and confirmed by other like-minded people.

Prophetic houses

Strong prophetic churches will activate and release large numbers of prophets and prophetic people because of a strong prophetic atmosphere conducive to nurturing and developing prophets. These churches will be strong in worship and prophecy, and they will have strong prophetic leaders to help mature emerging prophetic gifts.

Prophetic hubs

Many churches will become prophetic hubs for their cities and regions. A hub is a center of activity or interest; a focal point; a center around which other things revolve or from which they radiate. These hubs are places of encouragement, training, activation, and impartation for prophets and prophetic people. Ramah was a prophetic hub under the leadership of Samuel (1 Sam. 19:18–20).

Prophetic teams

Prophetic teams are good in helping young prophetic ministries work with more experienced prophetic ministers. This helps younger ministers develop and become stronger by being around those who are more mature and stronger. There is also an impartation that can be received, and valuable experience that helps people develop faith in ministering prophetically.

School of the prophets

It was under the administration of the Prophet/Judge Samuel, that we find the development of the school of the prophets. In this particular time period, about 1050–931 B.C., there were many false prophets that arose with false mediums of revelation. Samuel, who was raised as a boy by a priest named Eli, established training centers where young men would be taught the Law of Moses, responding to the Spirit of God and worship.

While one cannot be taught how to prophesy, the schools were geared to instruct the sons of the prophets how to flow with the Spirit when He came [upon] them.[8]

Prophetic caves

The church needs more Obadiah-type leaders. Obadiah protected, fed, and sheltered the prophets in caves when Jezebel was trying to destroy them. Some churches will have leaders with this Obadiah-type anointing, and they will become prophetic caves to hide, shelter, nourish, and protect prophets.

When Jezebel killed the prophets of the LORD, Obadiah took a hundred prophets and hid them in groups of fifty in a cave and fed them with bread and water.

—1 KINGS 18:4

Prophetic wildernesses

Many prophets are developed in the wilderness because there is no place for development in the church. John was developed in the wilderness. There was no place for him to be developed in the religious system of Jerusalem.

In those days John the Baptist came, preaching in the wilderness of Judea.

—MATTHEW 3:1

CORNELIUS CONNECTIONS: WHERE TO GO AND WHAT TO DO UPON BEING ACTIVATED

Then Peter went down to the men who were sent to him by Cornelius and said, "Here I am, the one you are seeking. Why have you come?" They said, "Cornelius, a centurion, a man who is righteous and fears God and is of good report throughout the nation of the Jews, was directed by a holy angel to summon you to his house to hear your words."

—ACTS 10:21–22

God will connect you with people who need the word of the Lord that is in your mouth.

Supernaturally people have dreamed my name and heard that they needed to contact me and have me pray for them and minister to them.

As you begin to activate and stir up your gift, God will begin to supernaturally connect you with people who need your anointing, who need the word of the Lord that is in your mouth.

This is the supernatural lifestyle God gives prophets and prophetic people. This is the exciting life of a prophet. I've found myself in cities and countries I never thought I'd be—places I've never heard of—but it was a divine connection because of the word I have in my mouth. And because I carry that prophetic anointing with me all the time, I was able to release the word of the Lord once I arrived there.

Some people want to be sent out to all kinds of places, but what word are they carrying that will take them into the place God has for them? Make sure you are consistently stirring up the gift that is within you so that you will be able to minister to people when they call.

There are 125 activations in this book that will get you well on your way to developing your gift to flow effectively in prophetic ministry. They can be followed in the order in which they are presented, or you can choose to follow them in an order based on the time element or, if you are studying in a group, what your leader desires to do. These activations will stretch you and give you the ability to operate in different dimensions of prophecy.

Chapter 1

BEGINNING ACTIVATIONS

Romans 12:6 says that there are many gifts in the body of Christ that are given through grace, but for prophecy it is given according to the proportion of faith. You must have a measure of faith in order to operate in the prophetic anointing. These beginning activations help to "prime the pump." They will help get the river to flow by increasing your measure of faith. Your faith must be accompanied by desire, as I mentioned above. You must desire to prophesy and then begin to stir up the gift of God within you, as it says in 2 Timothy 1:6. As the gift is stirred, it will begin to flow out of your belly (your spirit) like rivers of living water (John 7:38), bringing life to those who hear.

Now understand that these activations are not designed to teach you how to prophesy, per se, but how to hear from God and release what you hear. These activations are designed to encourage you to hear from God, listen to the Spirit, and step out in faith and get the river flowing. As you do that, you will develop your prophetic gift.

You will be challenged and stretched as you, by faith, embark on these activation exercises and dive deeper into the prophetic gift. As you get around others, there is a greater faith level, and that helps you launch out into the prophetic flow. Others can help you move in faith and by the Spirit of God.

Prophetic activation #1: read a scripture; release a prophetic word

In this activation you read or quote a verse of Scripture the Lord gives you for the person you are ministering to, and then you launch from that verse and minister prophetically to the person. This is a powerful exercise that will help your prophetic flow.

For example, 2 Timothy 1:7 says, "For God has not given us the spirit of fear…" You might hear the Lord say, "My son (or My daughter), don't be afraid; I am with You…"

Prophetic activation #2: receive one word; release a prophetic word

This activation is simple. When you stand before a person, believe God for just one word. It could be *grace, power, love,* or *mercy.* Launch from the one word God gives you into the prophetic flow. Sometimes God gives us one word, and as we speak prophetically, the word will expand and flow.

If the Lord gives you the word *power,* you might be led to say something like, "My son (or My daughter), My power is available to you. Don't be afraid to walk in My power. As you walk in power, you will see many miracles and breakthroughs in the days to come."

Prophetic activation #3: kick-start: pray in the Spirit; release a prophetic word

As you begin to minister, pray in the Spirit, allow the Lord to give you a word or a picture when you are praying, then launch into the prophetic flow. This tunes your spirit to what God wants to say to the person. Speaking in tongues is a good way to "kick-start" the prophetic flow.

Prophetic activation #4: see a picture; release a prophetic word

This exercise involves the seeing aspect of the prophetic anointing. Some people are more visionary. Ask the Lord for a picture, and launch into the prophetic word. This exercise will sharpen the visionary aspect of prophetic ministry. The pictures you can receive are limitless.

Prophetic activation #5: play music; sing a prophetic word

This activation requires music and will activate the prophetic song. Follow the music and sing prophetically to the person. Anointed music is a catalyst to the prophetic flow.

Prophetic activation #6: use an object; release a prophetic word

Common objects used in prophetic ministry include a watch, phone, keys, Bible, and so on. With an object in hand, launch into the prophetic flow. This activation will stretch your faith to speak into different areas of a person's life and increases the visual aspect of the prophetic flow.

Here are a few examples on how this could flow: 1) With a watch you may prophesy to the person concerning God's timing. 2) With a pen you may release a word about writing. 3) With keys you may release a word about God unlocking and opening doors for them, and so on.

Prophetic activation #7: bless the person; release a prophetic word

This activation begins with blessing the person you are ministering to. For example, you may say, "I bless you with…" peace, favor, shalom, and the like. Then you would launch into a prophetic word. You should hear a word when you are blessing them. This helps you flow into the power of prophetic blessing.

Prophetic activation #8: beginning with a "don't" word

This activation begins by speaking "don't." For example, "Don't be afraid," "Don't worry," "Don't be ashamed," or "Don't look back." This activation is an exercise in what God does not want us to do. The beginning of the prophetic word is with a "don't," and you launch into the prophecy and develop the word.

Prophetic activation #9: beginning with a question

Questions such as "Am I not your God?", "Am I not with you?", "Have I been faithful to you?", or "Have I not called you?" would begin an activation like this.

Sometimes the prophetic word begins with a question, and then the Lord speaks to us based on the question. In this activation you begin by allowing the Lord to give you a question for the person you are ministering to, and then you launch with a prophetic word.

> Have you not known? Have you not heard? Has it not been told to you from the beginning? Have you not understood from the foundations of the earth?
>
> —ISAIAH 40:21

Prophetic activation #10: "if" prophecies

These are prophecies that are conditional—"If you seek Me, then I will...," or "If you continue to worship Me, then I will..." "If you are faithful, then I will...," and so on.

This activation begins with an *if*. Ask the Lord to give you a word beginning with *if* for the person you are ministering to, and launch into the prophetic flow. This activation challenges the recipient to obey and be blessed.

> If you are willing and obedient, you shall eat the good of the land.
>
> —ISAIAH 1:19

Prophetic Protocol

1. Always prophesy in love. Love the people you minister to. Love is the motivation behind prophecy (1 Cor. 14:1). Do not prophesy out of bitterness, hurt, or anger. Love always seeks to edify. Love is not rude. Love is not harsh or condemning. Be sensitive to the person you are ministering to. Be polite.[1]

2. Prophesy according to your proportion of faith (Rom. 12:6). Do not copy others. Be yourself. God wants us all to be originals, not copies. We lose our own God-given individuality and uniqueness when we copy others. Strive to do your best and to be yourself.

3. Avoid being too demonstrative, dramatic, theatrical, or showy when ministering prophetically.

4. When ministering to a person of the opposite sex, do not lay your hands on any area of the person's body that could be considered sensitive. If you must touch, lay your hands gently on the head or on the shoulder. You may ask another person of the same sex as the recipient to place a hand on the person for the purpose of impartation and healing.

5. Do not allow people to worship you! Stay humble when people give praise and good reports about the ministry they received from you. Remember to worship Jesus. The testimony of Jesus is the spirit of prophecy (Rev. 19:10).

6. Don't be a prophetic "lone ranger." Learn to minister with others. We only know in part and prophesy in part. Submitting to others is a way to avoid pride. Prefer others when ministering. Do not be a prophetic "hog." Give others a chance to minister. Don't take up all the time. Learn to be a team player. A good follower makes a good leader.

7. Eliminate excessive hand motions, which distract the ministry recipient. This includes motions such as pointing, waving, and making fists. Also avoid rocking the person back and forth. Do not speak in tongues excessively while ministering prophetically. We can generally speak in tongues while beginning to get into the flow, but afterward stay with the known words of prophecy.

8. Never release a prophetic word that is contrary to the written Word of God. It is important for prophetic people to be students of the Word. Study to show yourself approved.

9. Know your strengths and limitations. Some people are stronger in certain areas of the prophetic anointing than others. Do not attempt to go beyond your measure of grace. We are not in a competition; we are not trying to outdo others.

10. Remember, the spirit of the prophet is subject to the prophet (1 Cor. 14:32). God does not give us something we cannot control. You should always have rule over your spirit (Prov. 25:28). Never allow things to get out of control.

11. Do not be repetitious while prophesying. This often happens when people speak too long. Stop when the Holy Spirit stops.

12. Use a recording device when possible. This will give the recipient the ability to write the prophecy down and review it. This avoids allowing the recipient to report that the minister said something he or she did not say, and it makes it possible for the prophecy to be judged by the leadership.

13. Speak in the first person. This may take time and practice to get accustomed to, but you are the voice of the Lord on the earth. This will result in a deeper flow prophetically.

Chapter 2
CREATIVE ACTIVATIONS

REATIVE ACTIVATIONS ARE designed to stretch you beyond the normal way you would hear and release a prophetic word. These are designed to have you prophesy on things you wouldn't normally prophesy on. Most people prophesy on hope, faith, and other words, but to prophesy on things such as "the ear" causes you to have to rely on the creativity and innovation of the Spirit. Prophets are, by nature, very creative and innovative. Those attributes are part of the prophet's mantle. God is the Creator, and He dwells in a place of new things and uncommon, divine creativity. He wants His prophets in that place with Him, ready to hear and act on His spontaneous word.

Prophetic activation #11: new thing prophecy
This activation begins with praying for God to do something new in the person's life you are ministering to. As you pray, believe God for a word that will release something new in the person's life, and then launch into the prophetic flow. You can prophesy new doors, new anointing, new relationships, new health, new revelation, and the like.

Prophecy is a powerful way to see the release of new things.

See, the former things have come to pass, and new things
I declare; before they spring forth I tell you of them.

—Isaiah 42:9

Prophetic activation #12: creation prophecies

This activation begins by asking God what He is cre-
ating for the person you are ministering to, or what they
have been created for (their purpose), and then launching
into the prophetic flow. God's Word is creative because
God is creative.

You have heard; see all this. And will you not declare it? I
have shown you new things from this time, even hidden
things, and you did not know them. They are created now
and not from the beginning; even before the day when you
did not hear them, lest you should say, "Yes, I knew them."

—Isaiah 48:6–7

But now, thus says the LORD who created you, O Jacob,
and He who formed you, O Israel: Do not fear, for I
have redeemed you; I have called you by your name; you
are Mine.

—Isaiah 43:1

Prophetic activation #13: prophesying in rhyme

This activation is designed to minster to the person
poetically. Prophecy can be poetic, which is a powerful
way to minster to people. Ask the Lord to give you a
rhyme for the person you are ministering to, and launch
into the prophetic flow. Take your time in this activation, and let the Holy Spirit give you the words. Here's
an example of what prophetic rhyme looks like:

I am with you today;
> don't be afraid.

I will go with you;
> your future I have made.

I speak to you today.
> You now hear My voice

Don't be sad.
> It is time to rejoice.

Prophetic activation #14: the ear

This activation focuses on the ear of the person you are ministering to. God often speaks to us concerning our ear (hearing). Touch the person's ear and pray for their spiritual hearing, and then launch into the prophetic word. Here are a couple examples of prophesying about someone's ear: "I am opening your ear to hear My voice," or "I am closing your ear to the voice of the enemy."

> Give ear, O my people, to my teaching: incline your ears to the words of my mouth.
>
> —PSALM 78:1

Prophetic activation #15: the eyes

This activation focuses on the eyes of the person you are ministering to. Pray for the person's eyes and ask the Lord to give you a word. Then launch into the prophetic word. The eyes are related to vision, discernment, revelation, insight, focus, etc.

> Your eyes shall see the King in His beauty; they shall see the land that is very far away.
>
> —ISAIAH 33:17

Prophetic activation #16: the mouth or tongue

This activation focuses on the mouth and tongue. Pray for the person's mouth and tongue, ask the Lord to give you a word, and then launch into the prophetic flow. Words for this prophetic activation can include preaching, teaching, singing, prophesying, praying, public speaking, wisdom, and the like.

> Then the lame man shall leap as a deer, and the tongue of the mute sing for joy. For in the wilderness waters shall break out and streams in the desert.
>
> —Isaiah 35:6

Prophetic activation #17: the hands

Hold the person by the hand and pray for their hands while asking the Lord to give you a word; then launch into the prophetic flow. Examples of words given during this activation can include healing hands, God holding their hands, God lifting their hands, God using their hands, and the like.

> Thus says the Lord to Cyrus, His anointed, whose right hand I have held—to subdue nations before him and to loosen the loins of kings, to open before him so that the gates will not be shut.
>
> —Isaiah 45:1

Prophetic activation #18: the heart

This activation focuses on the person's heart, their innermost being. Pray for the person's heart, and ask the Lord to show you their heart. When you receive a word, launch into the prophetic word. Words here can include a pure heart, new heart, courageous heart, healing your heart, and the like.

> Say to those who are of a fearful heart, "Be strong, fear not. Your God will come with vengeance, even God with a recompense; He will come and save you."
> —ISAIAH 35:4

Prophetic activation #19: the mind

Lay your hand on the person's head and pray for their mind and thought life. Ask the Lord to give you a word for their mind and thoughts, and launch into the prophetic word. Words can include knowledge, intelligence, creativity, order, restoration, and the like.

> Search me, O God, and know my heart: try me, and know my thoughts.
> —PSALM 139:23, KJV

Prophetic activation #20: the feet

Pray for the feet of the person. The feet represent the person's walk, path, and journey. Ask the Lord to give you a word, and launch into the prophetic flow. Words that can be released during this kind of activation can include new feet, beautiful feet, new path, different path, travel, and so on.

> So I prophesied as He commanded me, and the breath came into them, and they lived and stood up upon their feet, an exceeding great army.
> —EZEKIEL 37:10

Chapter 3

ACTIVATIONS PROMPTED BY THE NAMES OF GOD

T HE FOLLOWING ACTIVATIONS are released from the name of God. God drops His word when we publish the name of the Lord. In Deuteronomy 32:2–3, the Bible says, "My teaching will drop [Hebrew word *nataph* meaning 'to prophesy'] like the rain, my sayings will distill as the dew, as the droplets on the grass, and as the showers on the herb. For I will proclaim the name of the LORD: Ascribe greatness to our God!"

Prophetic activation #21: Jehovah Jireh

This activation launches on the name *Jehovah Jireh* (the Lord My Provider). God drops His word (*nataph*— "to drop," "to prophesy") when we publish His name and ascribe greatness to Him. Ascribe greatness to the name Jehovah Jireh by verbally declaring His greatness, allow and wait for God to drop His word, then launch into the prophetic flow. Possible prophetic words that flow out of this activation include challenges to give, to trust, or to have faith in God's provision. In Genesis 22:14 we see that Jehovah Will Provide is the name given by Abraham to the place where he had almost slayed his son Isaac.

Prophetic activation #22: Jehovah Rapha

This activation launches on the name *Jehovah Rapha* (the Lord My Healer). This is a great way to release a healing word that can include physical or inner healing. God brought Israel to Marah, the place where the Lord became known as "the Lord who heals you" (Exod. 15:26). He brought them here to teach them and to make Himself known to them. He causes us to reflect back on that place to teach us and make Himself known to us as our healer. (See 1 Corinthians 10:11.)

For example, you may hear the Lord say to you on behalf of the person, "Son/daughter, I am your healer. I am healing you now from the past, binding up your wounds, and causing new life to flow through your mind, body, and spirit. You don't have to wonder; it is My desire to bring healing to every area of your life that is hurting."

Prophetic activation #23: Jehovah Shalom

The name *Jehovah Shalom* means "the Lord My Peace." The peace of God, or shalom, includes prosperity, health, and wholeness. The words launched from this activation will bring peace and wholeness to those you minister to. Gideon named the place where God confirmed his victory over the Midianites "The Lord Is Peace," and he built an altar there (Judg. 6:24).

You may be led to say something like this: "My son/My daughter, I am your peace. Cast your cares upon Me. My peace I give to you. I don't give you peace that the world gives. You will have My peace that passes all understanding. Let not your heart be troubled."

Prophetic activation #24: Jehovah Shammah

Jehovah Shammah means "the Lord Is Present." These words confirm the presence of God with a person and the benefits of his presence. Jehovah Shammah is a Christian transliteration of the Hebrew, meaning "Jehovah is there," the name given to the city in Ezekiel's vision in Ezekiel 48:35.

For this activation you may hear the Lord say something like, "My son/My daughter, I am with you. I am in the midst of your troubles. I am in the midst of your storm. I am with you even until the end."

Prophetic activation #25: El Shaddai

El Shaddai means "Mighty God." These words can speak of God's power and might in a person's life and release faith to believe for God's mighty acts. In the Old Testament El Shaddai occurs seven times and is first used in Genesis 17:1.

An example of what this activation may release may be something like this: "My son/My daughter, get ready to see Me perform mighty acts in your life. Get ready to see a move of My power over your situation. I am Almighty God."

Prophetic activation #26: I AM

I AM THAT I AM was revealed to Moses. This name of God provides an unlimited number of words that can be released through revealing who God is to the person you are ministering to. You could begin by declaring to the person that God is their shield, deliverer, healer, provider, friend, and so on, as the Lord reveals to you His position in the person's life.

When Moses saw the burning bush in the desert, he asked God, "When they say to me, 'What is His name?' what shall I say to them?" (Exod. 3:13). God answered his question by the revelation of His name as the "I Am." "And God said to Moses, 'I AM WHO I AM,' and He said, 'You will say this to the children of Israel, "I AM has sent me to you"'" (v. 14).

Prophetic activation #27: Jehovah M'Kaddesh

This name means "the God Who Sanctifies." A God separate from all that is evil requires that the people who follow Him be cleansed from all evil. This activation is launched with a word of sanctification, holiness, and separation.

> Speak also to the children of Israel, saying, "You must surely keep My Sabbaths, for it is a sign between Me and you throughout your generations, that you may know that I am the LORD who sanctifies you."
>
> —EXODUS 31:13

An example of a word launched from this activation may be something like, "My son/My daughter, I am sanctifying you, making you holy, and setting you apart for My use. Let Me purify you so that you may be holy. Let Me wash you so that you may be clean."

Prophetic activation #28: Jehovah Nissi

Jehovah Nissi means "the Lord My Banner." Words of victory and triumph are released through this activation.

Then Moses built an altar and called the name of it, The
LORD Is My Banner;

—EXODUS 17:15

An example of a word released from this activation is,
"I am your banner. Be encouraged, for today I am giving
you victory over all your enemies. By the power of My
name you have overcome."

Prophetic activation #29: Jehovah Rohi

Jehovah Rohi means "the Lord My Shepherd." In this
activation you would be challenged to release words that
speak of the Lord's protection, leading, feeding, and the
like. The most extensive reference to the Lord as our
shepherd is Psalm 23.

Prophetic activation #30: Wonderful

God is a God of wonders. This activation will cause
you to speak words that tell of the wonderful works
of God in the life of the person you are ministering to.
Wonderful means "inspiring delight, pleasure, or admira-
tion; extremely good; marvelous."

Names of God

- El Shaddai (Lord God Almighty)—Genesis 17:1; 28:3;
  35:11; 43:14; 48:3

- El Elyon (The Most High God)—Genesis 14:18–19, 20,
  22; Psalm 57:2; 78:35

- Adonai (Lord, Master)—In the Old Testament *Adonai*
  occurs 434 times. There are heavy uses of *Adonai* in
  Isaiah as "Adonai Jehovah." It occurs two hundred times

in Ezekiel alone and appears eleven times in Daniel chapter 9. *Adonai* is first used in Genesis 15:2.[1]

- Yahweh (Lord, Jehovah)—Used more than any other name of God, Yahweh occurs in the Old Testament more than five thousand times. It is first used in Genesis 2:4.[2]

- Jehovah Nissi (The Lord My Banner)—Exodus 17:15

- Jehovah-Raah (The Lord My Shepherd)—Psalm 23; also Jehovah Rohi or Jehovah Ro'eh

- Jehovah Rapha (The Lord That Heals)—Exodus 15:26

- Jehovah Shammah (The Lord Is There)—Ezekiel 48:35

- Jehovah Tsidkenu (The Lord Our Righteousness)—Jeremiah 23:6; 33:16

- Jehovah Mekoddishkem (The Lord Who Sanctifies You)—Exodus 31:13; Leviticus 20:8; also Jehovah M'Kaddesh

- El Olam (The Everlasting God)—Genesis 21:33; Isaiah 26:4; Jeremiah 10:10

- Elohim (God)—In the Old Testament *Elohim* occurs over two thousand times. *Elohim* is first used in Genesis 1:1.[3]

- Qanna (Jealous)—Exodus 20:5; 34:14; Deuteronomy 4:24; 5:9; 6:15

- Jehovah Jireh (The Lord Will Provide)—Genesis 22:14

- Jehovah Shalom (The Lord Is Peace)—Judges 6:24

- Jehovah Sabaoth (The Lord of Hosts)—1 Samuel 1:11; 17:45; 2 Samuel 6:18; 7:27; 1 Kings 19:14; 2 Kings 3:14; 1 Chronicles 11:9; Psalm 24:10; 48:8; 80:4, 19; 84:3; Isaiah 1:24; 3:15; 5:16; 6:5; 9:19; 10:26; 14:22; Jeremiah 9:15; 48:1; Hosea 12:5; Amos 3:13; Micah 4:4; Nahum 3:5; Habakkuk 2:13; Zephaniah 2:9; Haggai 2:6; Zechariah 1:3; Malachi 1:6

Chapter 4

ACTIVATIONS PROMPTED BY SPIRITUAL VIRTUES

GOD OFTEN CHALLENGES us through the prophetic word in the areas of spiritual virtues such as love, faith, hope, or holiness. These areas are very important to a believer. The word of the Lord will often challenge, encourage, and help in these areas of our lives, causing us to be strong and fully developed. These kinds of words are very important for a believer to hear from the Lord. Some people need to be healed, corrected, or refocused on these areas. The prophetic word will do that. Some people also need to be commended in these areas. The word of the Lord will come and let them know that they are doing well.

Prophetic activation #31: love

Focus on the love of God for the person you are ministering to. Speak words of love over the person, and launch into the prophetic flow. These words remind people of the love of God for them and challenge them to walk in love, compassion, and forgiveness. This activation releases the prophetic minister to operate in the love of God in the prophetic flow.

Anyone who does not love does not know God, for God is love.

—1 JOHN 4:8

Prophetic activation #32: faith

Focus on the area of faith, speak words concerning faith, and then launch into the prophetic word. Faith is an important part of the believer's life, and God will often speak to us and challenge us in this area. These words challenge people in the area of faith and exhort them to remove doubt and unbelief from their lives.

And without faith it is impossible to please God, for he who comes to God must believe that He exists and that He is a rewarder of those who diligently seek Him.

—HEBREWS 11:6

Prophetic activation #33: mercy

Focus on the mercy of God. Speak the mercy of God over the person you are ministering to, and then launch into the prophetic word. These words remind people of God's mercy and forgiveness and deliver them from guilt, condemnation, and shame. This activation helps the prophetic minister to operate in the mercy and compassion of the Lord when ministering.

Oh, give thanks unto the LORD, for He is good, for His mercy endures forever!

—PSALM 107:1

Prophetic activation #34: hope

Focus on the subject of hope, and pray over the person's hopes and dreams; then launch into the prophetic word. Use this word to stir people to hope and dream. This activation helps the prophetic minister release hope and encouragement.

> Now may the God of hope fill you with all joy and peace in believing, so that you may abound in hope, through the power of the Holy Spirit.
>
> —ROMANS 15:13

Prophetic activation #35: holiness

Pray for the person's holiness and sanctification, and launch into the prophetic word. These words challenge people to walk in purity and to remove impurities from their lives. This activation helps the prophetic minister stand for righteousness and purity.

> Pursue peace with all men, and the holiness without which no one will see the Lord.
>
> —HEBREWS 12:14

Prophetic activation #36: power

Pray for the person to walk in the power of God, and then launch into the prophetic word. These words challenge people to walk in power and demonstration of the Spirit. This activation reminds the prophetic minister that the prophetic ministry is not in word only but also in power. Sometimes the power of God is released during this activation to release a miracle in the life of the person ministered to.

He gives power to the faint, and to those who have no
might He increases strength.

—Isaiah 40:29

Prophetic activation #37: authority

Focus on the authority of the believer through Christ,
pray for the authority of Christ to increase, and launch
into the prophetic word. These words exhort people to
walk in and exercise their authority in Christ. This activation also increases the authority in which the prophetic
minister prophesies.

Then He called His twelve disciples together and gave
them power and authority over all demons and to cure
diseases.

—Luke 9:1

Prophetic activation #38: humility

Focus on the virtue of humility, pray for the person
to walk in humility, and launch into the prophetic flow.
These words exhort people to walk in humility and warn
against the dangers of pride. This activation reminds
the prophetic minister of the virus of pride versus the
anointing that comes with humility—and the need for
the anointing, especially in prophecy.

Likewise you younger ones, submit yourselves to the
elders. Yes, all of you be submissive one to another and
clothe yourselves with humility, because "God resists
the proud, but gives grace to the humble."

—1 Peter 5:5

Prophetic activation #39: joy

Focus on the joy of the Lord (you can even laugh during this activation) and launch into the prophetic flow. These words remind people of the importance of joy and come against situations that steal joy. This activation releases the prophetic minister to minister the prophetic word with joy.

> Then he said to them, "Go your way. Eat the fat, drink the sweet drink, and send portions to those for whom nothing is prepared; for this day is holy to our Lord. Do not be grieved, for the joy of the LORD is your strength."
>
> —NEHEMIAH 8:10

Prophetic activation #40: favor

Focus on the favor of God, speak favor over the person's life, and launch into the prophetic flow. These words release the favor of God for blessing and promotion. This impartation helps the prophetic minister release favor.

> For You, LORD, will bless the righteous; You surround him with favor like a shield.
>
> —PSALM 5:12

Chapter 5

TEAM MINISTRY ACTIVATIONS

PROPHETS CAN ALSO work together in teams. Teams help keep prophets balanced, and teamwork provides a healthy barrier against pride, isolation, and exclusiveness. We have many recognized prophets in our local assembly, and they understand that teamwork is the way to go. We need to be connected with people who flow strongly in prophetic ministry.

The following activations are for training prophets and prophetic people in how to minister in groups of three or with the help of a more experienced prophetic minister.

Prophetic activation #41: follow the prophetic word of another (piggyback)

This activation will pair you with someone who is stronger and more experienced in the prophetic ministry. This will help you receive an impartation as you work with this partner, who can evaluate your prophetic flow and help you overcome any obstacles or challenges you experience as you begin to operate in the prophetic anointing.

In this activation you will allow the more experienced person to go first in ministry, and then you will follow (piggyback) in ministering to the person. Listen carefully to your partner minister, and allow the Holy Spirit to highlight a word or a phrase that is released, then launch into the prophetic flow based on what the Holy Spirit highlights to you. You will simply move in the flow and strength of what has been released. Don't be intimidated. Simply speak what the Lord gives you after your partner turns the ministry over to you.

Prophetic activation #42: initiate the prophetic word and then follow

In this activation you will go first, and the more experienced person will follow and expand on what you minister. This activation will help you see how much deeper the word that you began can go. You will then follow with a word that continues to expand what you originally began. This activation will teach you that prophetic ministry is like a river that continues to flow.

Prophetic activation #43: receive an impartation, then prophesy

In this activation the more experienced prophetic person lays hands on you and releases an impartation by faith, then releases you to minister to the person. After receiving the impartation, launch into the prophetic flow and believe for a stronger release.

Prophetic activation #44: prophesy to the other prophetic minister, then to the third party

In this activation you will pray for the more experienced prophetic minister and encourage him/her with a word. After you finishing sharing with that person, turn and minister to the other person. This will stretch you to minister to more than one person.

Prophetic activation #45: receive a word and release a word

In this activation you allow the more experienced prophetic minister to minister to you, and then you will turn and minister to the other person. This activation will stir you because after you receive a word, you will be inspired to release a word.

Prophetic activation #46: insight from the more experienced minister

In this activation ask the more experienced prophetic minister for any instruction that can help you in your prophetic flow. The more experienced prophetic minister should be able to assist you in any adjustments you need to make, and then release you to minister again.

Prophetic activation #47: start, stop, start

In this activation you will start by praying and ministering to the third party, and when the more experienced minister says stop, you will stop, and then turn to the experienced minister and start to minster to them. When the minister says stop, you will then turn to the other person and resume ministering to them until you are told to stop. This activation helps you to understand that the spirit of the prophet is subject to the prophet and that you can resume in the prophetic flow. (See 1 Corinthians 14:32.)

Prophetic activation #48: minister to both

In this activation, have the other two hold hands, pray over them, and release a word to both at the same time. In other words, you are believing for a word that applies to both of them. This is a mini-corporate word. This helps to move you into the corporate flow. Some words are for individuals, and some are for groups.

Prophetic activation #49: release a word to the minister after they share

You will allow the more experienced minister to minister to the third party, and when he or she has finished, you will prophesy to the minister.

Your prophetic flow should be stronger by now, and the minister after receiving will minster to you. The word is usually an encouragement to you in your prophetic adventure. This also can be a time of more impartation from the more experienced minister.

Prophetic activation #50: release a word to the experienced minister and then the third party again—twice

You will begin by praying for and launching into the prophetic flow beginning with the more experienced minister, then when the minister says, "Switch," you will turn and begin ministering to the third party. The experienced minister will say, "Switch," again, and you will return to ministering prophetically to the experienced minister. The minister will say, "Switch," again and you will return to ministering to the third party. This activation will stretch you with the help of a more experienced prophetic minister.

The Blessing of Prophetic Impartation

One of the abilities of prophets is to impart blessings to other people. We see this in Romans 1:11, where the apostle Paul said, "For I long to see you, that I may impart unto you some spiritual gift, to the end ye may be established" (KJV). Paul had a desire to come to the church at Rome so that he could impart spiritual gifts to the church members and help them be established in mature strength. It was the anointing of the prophet that gave him the ability to impart spiritual gifts and anointings into people through prophetic utterances and through the laying on of hands.

Timothy received an impartation of a gift and the anointing of God through prophecy and the laying on of hands: "Neglect not the gift that is in thee, which was given thee by prophecy, with the laying on of the hands of the presbytery" (1 Tim. 4:14, KJV).

There was a transference of spiritual power, authority, ability, and grace. Paul then told Timothy not to neglect what he had received through impartation.

All of us need impartations of the anointing. You can receive some things directly from God; other things will come through the channel of another individual. Although most people received gifts and callings when they were born again and baptized in the Holy Spirit, additional anointings can come through the avenue of laying on of hands and prophecy.

When this avenue is lacking, the result will be a lack of strong ministries and anointings in the local assembly. We need this blessing of impartation, given to us by the Lord Jesus Christ. It is important that the body of Christ discern and embrace this function of prophets. Otherwise, we will miss the deposit of anointings and gifts that could have come through prophetic impartation. All who operate in ministry gifts, especially those who are young, can benefit from receiving additional supernatural gifts and anointings through prophesying and praying with the laying on of hands.

According to Romans 1:11, the result of this impartation is establishment. You can be established, firm and strong, in your ministry as the prophets impart unto you through prophecy and the laying on of hands.[1]

Chapter 6

BIBLE ACTIVATIONS

I N ORDER TO take advantage of these next activations, you must have some basic knowledge about what different Bible symbols mean. These may be more for intermediate or advanced prophetic people who have had more time in the Word. It's important to understand that the Bible is a prophetic book and is full of prophetic symbols to launch from.

Prophetic activation #51: Bible names

The names of people in the Bible are very prophetic, and the Lord will often give a person a word using people in the Bible. The most common are Abraham, Joseph, Moses, Joshua, Samuel, David, Elijah, and Esther.

Begin this activation by praying for the person and asking the Lord to give you a Bible name; then launch into the prophetic flow. Even Jezebel can come up in referring to someone being delivered from the attacks of Jezebel. This activation will help the prophetic minister be open to God's use of names as symbols while prophesying. It is also possible to prophesy a new name over a person.

Prophetic activation #52: books of the Bible

Each book of the Bible carries a message or theme. For example:

+ Genesis—the beginning
+ Psalms—praise
+ Proverbs—wisdom
+ Galatians—liberty
+ Revelation—the kingdom

Pray for the person, and ask the Lord to give you a book of the Bible; then launch into the prophetic flow. This will require some basic knowledge of the books of the Bible. Sometimes you will call out the person's favorite Bible book or even encourage them to study a certain book.

Prophetic activation #53: Bible minerals

God will often use minerals or elements (gold, silver, brass, diamond, ruby, emerald, wood) to give a message. Pray for the person and ask God to give you a mineral, and then launch into the prophetic flow. This will require a basic knowledge of minerals, their meaning, and how they are referenced in the Bible.

Prophetic activation #54: Bible colors

Colors are also prophetic. Bible colors include:

+ Purple—royalty
+ White—purity
+ Red—redemption

- Green—prosperity
- Black—mystery, hidden
- Blue—heavenly

Pray for the person and ask the Lord to give you a Bible color; then launch into the prophetic word. This activation will help the prophetic minister be open to God giving colors as symbols when prophesying.

Prophetic activation #55: Bible numbers

Numbers are also prophetic. Common biblical numbers include:

- One—beginning, God
- Two—double, witness, agreement
- Five—grace, goodness, favor
- Seven—completion
- Eight—new beginning
- Twelve—government, apostolic authority
- Thirteen—rebellion, lawlessness
- Forty—testing, trial, generation
- Fifty—jubilee, freedom, Holy Spirit, Pentecost
- One thousand—perfection

Ask the Lord to give you a Bible number, and launch into the prophetic flow. This activation will help the prophetic ministry be open to God showing numbers when ministering.

Prophetic activation #56: Bible elements

Elements are strong symbols of the prophetic anointing. These include wind, fire, water, and earth. Pray for the person, asking the Lord to give you one of these elements, and launch into the prophetic flow. This can also include rivers, mountains, and storms.

Prophetic activation #57: Bible creatures

Eagles, lions, horses, hawks, ants, serpents, wolves, sheep, and others can all be prophetic symbols. Pray for the person, ask the Lord to give you a Bible creature, and launch into the prophetic flow. Each animal has a certain characteristic—even a serpent can be a picture of wisdom. This activation will help the prophetic minister be open to receive animals as symbols when ministering.

Prophetic activation #58: Bible miracles

There are many miracles in the Bible that have prophetic messages. One of my favorites is Lazarus being raised from the dead. Miracles of healing, deliverance, and provision are abundant in Scripture. Pray for the person, ask the Lord to give you a Bible miracle, and launch into the prophetic flow.

Prophetic activation #59: Bible sounds

Sounds like the sound of wind blowing, rain falling, praise, joy, war, trumpets, shouting, and clapping can also be prophetic. Pray for the person, listen as a sound is released in your ear, and launch into the prophetic flow. This activation will break the limitation of the prophetic minister from just hearing a word or seeing a picture.

Prophetic activation #60: Bible prophets

Each Bible prophet is unique and symbolizes a different aspect of the prophetic ministry. There are also lesser-known prophets such as Asaph, Heman, and Jeduthun—all musical prophets. There are also governmental prophets such as Daniel. Elijah, Isaiah, Ezekiel, Jeremiah, and John are prophets most believers are familiar with. Pray for the person, ask the Lord to give you a biblical prophet, and launch into the prophetic flow.

Bible Prophets—Names and Meanings

- Amos—"burden bearer"
- Anna—"favor" or "grace"
- Asaph—"convener" or collector"
- Barnabas—"son of consolation"
- Daniel—"God is my Judge"
- David—"beloved"
- Elijah—"whose God is Jehovah"
- Elisha—"God his salvation"
- Ezekiel—"dedication"
- Gad—"fortune"
- Habakkuk—"God will strengthen"
- Haggai—"embrace"
- Heman—"faithful"
- Hosea—"salvation"
- Isaiah—"festive"
- Jeduthun—"lauder" or "praising"

- Jeremiah—"raised up or appointed by Jehovah"
- Joel—"Jehovah is his God"
- Jonah—"a dove"
- Malachi—"messenger" or "angel"
- Micah—"who is like Jehovah"
- Micaiah—"who is like Jah"
- Nahum—"consolation"
- Nathan—"gift from God"
- Obadiah—"servant of the Lord"
- Samuel—"heard of God"
- Zechariah—"Jehovah is renowned or remembered"
- Zephaniah—"the Lord conceals"

As we eat the Lord, enjoy Him, drink Him, breathe Him in, and meet with the saints, there's something bubbling in us, some words that are coming out of us for building up! As we practice to speak in the meetings again and again, we are perfected in our prophesying for the building up of the church as the Body of Christ.[1]

—STEFAN MISARAS

Chapter 7

PROPHETIC PRAYER ACTIVATIONS

THIS NEXT SET of activations are some of the easiest activations to do because everybody can pray. Prayer is like a bridge into prophetic ministry. These prophetic prayer activations serve as a foundation to launch into the prophetic flow. These activations help the minister to pray prophetically. Often when you are praying for people, God will begin to give you a word for them. Learning to pray prophetically is basically praying what God is revealing to you at the time. This is spontaneous-type prayer, or praying by inspiration, then releasing what God is saying.

Prophetic activation #61: finances

This activation includes praying prophetically for the person's finances. Allow the Holy Spirit to give you what to pray. You may be inspired to pray for increase, business, saving, adjustments, debt, investments, new job, new career, and the like. You can then launch into the prophetic word concerning their finances.

Prophetic activation #62: health

This activation includes praying for someone's health. Allow the Holy Spirit to give you what to pray. You may be inspired to pray for healing, strength, restoration, rest, stress, eating habits, tiredness, and other things that affect a person's health. You can then launch into the prophetic flow.

Prophetic activation #63: ministry

This activation includes praying for the person's place in the body of Christ. Focusing on Romans 12, Ephesians 4, and 1 Corinthians 12—the chapters in the Bible that outline the gifts and ministries of the Spirit—allow the Holy Spirit to give you what to pray. You can be inspired to pray for their ministry, calling, gifts (revelation, power, utterance), and anointing. You can then launch into the prophetic flow.

Prophetic activation #64: family

This activation includes praying for the person's family. Allow the Holy Spirit to give you what to pray. You can be inspired to pray for salvation, unity, marriages, children, men, women, and other things related to the family. You can then launch into the prophetic flow.

Prophetic activation #65: city

This activation includes praying for the city the person is from. Allow the Lord to give you what to pray. You may be inspired to pray for the economy, educational system, youth, churches, spiritual climate, and so on. You can then launch into the prophetic flow.

Prophetic activation #66: destiny

This activation includes praying for the person's destiny and future. Allow the Lord to give you what to pray. You may be inspired to pray for his/her purpose, path, decisions, relationships, doors, career, and so on. You can then launch into the prophetic flow.

Prophetic activation #67: relationships

This activation includes praying for the person's relations. Allow the Lord to give you what to pray. You may be inspired to pray for new relationships, old relationships, broken relationships, restored relationships, bad relationships, and the like. You can then launch into the prophetic flow.

Prophetic activation #68: marital status

This activation includes praying for the person's marital status (married, single, or divorced). Allow the Lord to give you what to pray. You may be inspired to pray for restoration, patience, healing, blessing, and the like. You can then launch into the prophetic flow.

Prophetic activation #69: career

This activation includes praying for the person's career. Allow the Lord to give you what to pray. You may be inspired to pray for promotion, a new career, employment, change in career, education, and the like. You can then launch into the prophetic flow.

Prophetic activation #70: dream and vision

This activation includes praying for the person's dreams and vision for his/her life. Allow the Lord to give you what to pray. You may be inspired to pray for a wide variety of things because there are so many different dreams and hopes that people carry. You can then launch into the prophetic flow.

Effective and Inspired Prayer

When you base your prayers on the Word of God, it will inspire you to pray. Praying the Word of God will expand your ability to pray. It will stir up a spirit of prayer within you. We are told to pray with all kinds of prayers (Eph. 6:18). Praying the Word will cause you to pray many different kinds of prayers that you ordinarily would not have prayed. This will help to break the limitations off your prayer life. Reading, studying, and meditating on the promises of God will motivate you to pray. God has given many great and precious promises—promises to help you, to save and deliver you from the hand of the enemy, and to heal you and prosper you. It is through faith-filled prayer that you inherit these covenant promises (Heb. 6:12).

Prayer is also one of the ways we release the will of God upon the earth. We must study the Word of God in order to know the will of God. This is why prayer and the Word must be combined. Daniel was able to pray effectively because he knew the Word of God concerning His people (Dan. 9:2–3).

We should pray with understanding (1 Cor. 14:15). Understanding the will of God will help us pray correctly. The Word of God is the will of God. We are not to be unwise; we are to understand what the will of the Lord is (Eph. 5:17). Prayer also helps us walk perfectly and completely in all the will of God (Col. 4:12).

We are encouraged to call upon the Lord. He has promised to show us great and mighty things (Jer. 33:3). The Lord delights in our prayers. He delights in answering our prayers. Before we call, He will answer (Isa. 65:24). The Lord's ears are open unto the prayers of the righteous (1 Pet. 3:12). The effectual fervent prayer of a righteous man avails much (James 5:16). We are told to pray without ceasing (1 Thess. 5:17).

Our God hears prayer. All flesh should come to Him in prayer (Ps. 65:2). All believers have similar challenges, and all believers can overcome these challenges through prayer. God is no respecter of persons. He is near to all who call upon Him (Ps. 145:19). The Lord will hear your supplication and will receive your prayers (Ps. 6:9). Calling upon the Lord will bring salvation and deliverance from your enemies (Ps. 18:3). This has always been a key to deliverance. You can pray yourself out of any adverse situation. The Lord is your helper. God will not turn away your prayers (Ps. 66:20). God will not despise your prayers (Ps. 102:17). The prayers of the upright are God's delight (Prov. 15:8).[1]

Chapter 8

PROPHETIC SONGS AND WORSHIP ACTIVATIONS

THESE ACTIVATIONS REQUIRE singing. You do not have to be a great singer to participate. Prophecy can be spoken or sung. These activations will help the prophetic minister flow in the various songs of the Lord. Every praise and worship team should be activated this way. The song of the Lord is simply the Lord Jesus singing through us to the person, revealing His heart to them. Prophetic songs are powerful because they go deep into the heart of the recipient.

Prophetic activation #71: new song

This activation is simple and requires you to sing a new song. Ask the Lord for a melody or follow a minstrel, and launch into the prophetic song.

Prophetic activation #72: song of love

This is simply a love song from the Lord to the person you are ministering to. Speak the love of God over the person, and launch into the prophetic flow. Allow the Lord to sing about His love for the person through your voice.

Prophetic activation #73: song of encouragement

This song is to encourage the person. Ask the Lord what area the person needs encouragement in, and launch into a prophetic song of encouragement. Allow the Lord to sing through you a song of encouragement.

Prophetic activation #74: song of healing

Ask the Lord what areas the person needs healing in—physical, emotional, the past, and the like—and launch into a prophetic song of healing. Miracles of healing can occur through this activation. Also, this activation trains the minister to be sensitive in this area of ministering to the hurts and pains of people.

Prophetic activation #75: song of deliverance

Ask the Lord what area the person may need deliverance in—hurt, fear, rejection, unforgiveness, and so on. Use wisdom in this area, for there may be things you do not have to call out by name, and then launch into the prophetic song about freedom, liberation, chains being broken, feet untied, or whatever the Lord leads you to sing to bring deliverance to the person's life. God sends His word to heal and deliver (Ps. 107:20).

> Thou art my hiding place; thou shalt preserve me from trouble; thou shalt compass me about with songs of deliverance. Selah.
>
> —PSALM 32:7, KJV

Prophetic activation #76: song of commendation

This song commends what the person is doing right or well. Ask the Lord in what areas He wants to commend the person, and then launch into the prophetic song. God often speaks well over us through the prophetic song.

Prophetic activation #77: song of victory

The Prophetess Miriam sang a song of victory after coming through the Red Sea (Exod. 15:20–21). Ask the Lord in what area He wants to bring victory to the person's life, and launch into the prophetic song. This song will celebrate the victory of the Lord in the person's life.

Prophetic activation #78: song of ascent

Songs of Ascent (Psalms 120–134) were songs that Israel sang when they were ascending to Jerusalem to worship. This song calls the person to move up higher in different areas of their life. Ask the Lord in what areas He wants the person to come higher—faith, hope, love, worship, prayer, holiness—and launch into the prophetic song. This song will challenge the person to ascend into a new place.

Prophetic activation #79: scripture song

This is simply singing over the person from the Scriptures. Select a scripture that the Lord lays on your heart and begin to sing it over the person, and then launch from there into the prophetic song. This trains the prophetic minister to be open to using Scripture in singing the song of the Lord.

Thy statutes have been my songs in the house of my pilgrimage.

—PSALM 119:54, KJV

Prophetic activation #80: song of restoration

Ask the Lord what area the person may need restoration in (e.g., finances, health, relationships, family, ministry); then speak restoration over them and allow the Lord to sing through you a song of restoration. Much of the prophetic ministry has to do with restoration, and this activation will train the prophetic minister to be a vessel of restoration.

THE CASE FOR WORSHIPPING PROPHETS

As I stated in *Prophet, Arise!*, we need more than musicians; we need prophet musicians who release the sound of heaven on earth. We see examples of prophet musicians in 1 Chronicles 25:1.

> Then David and the officers of the army also set apart for the service some of the sons of Asaph, and of Heman, and of Jeduthun, those who prophesied with lyres, harps, and cymbals. The number of those who did the work according to their service was.

Singing prophets

John and Jesus ministered to Israel in different ways. Prophetic ministry is like a song. John came singing a dirge (a song of mourning). Jesus came playing a wedding song. Israel did not respond to either.

Prophets require a response. Prophets release a sound and a song. What are the prophets singing and playing?

> We piped to you [playing wedding], and you did not dance; we wailed dirges [playing funeral], and you did not mourn and beat your breasts and weep aloud.
>
> —MATTHEW 11:17, AMPC

Dancing prophets

Both Miriam and David expressed themselves in the dance. Prophets are expressive, and the dance is one of the most powerful ways to express God's power, victory, love, and mercy.

> Miriam the prophetess, the sister of Aaron, took a timbrel in her hand, and all the women went out after her with timbrels and with dancing.
>
> —EXODUS 15:20

> David danced before the LORD with all of his might, and he wore a linen ephod.
>
> —2 SAMUEL 6:14

Nataph—Prophetic Worship

> The earth shook; the heavens also dropped rain at the presence of God; Sinai itself was moved at the presence of God, the God of Israel.
>
> —PSALM 68:8, NKJV

Dropped in the above verse is the Hebrew word *nataph*, which means "to drop, drip, distill, distill gradually, prophesy, preach, discourse, to ooze." The Lord drops His prophetic word. This word drops from heaven. This is the result of the presence of the Lord. This happens during worship. God inhabits the praises of His people. The presence of the Lord will manifest as a result of praise. The presence of God causes us to worship. Worship is our response to His presence.

God drops the prophetic song. The singers can sing prophetically as a result of *nataph*. These are songs from heaven. They are dropped from heaven. These songs can drop on anyone in the congregation.

Nataph is sometimes translated "prophet," which means "to drop, drip, or distill." Its uses include rain distilling and dripping from the sky, words that "drop" out of someone's mouth, and wine dripping from the mountains in paradise.

Another Hebrew word translated "prophet" shows that prophets speak what they hear from God (or today from the Lord Jesus), and they do not speak on their own. Although prophets are called upon to "drop" words where and when God demands, the more obvious thing we learn from *nataph* is that God drops His words upon the prophet. According to *Strong's*, it means, "to speak by inspiration." This means that the message the prophet brings is not his own message, but the Lord's words; furthermore, it implies that many times the prophet may not know much of the message when he starts prophesying, but that the words "drop" upon him, that is, he speaks them as he gets them from God.

This dropping causes us to sing inspired songs. Songs of inspiration are prophetic songs. The singer is inspired by God to sing a new song. Churches must allow God to drop these songs during worship. We should not quench the manifestation of the Spirit (1 Thess. 5:19).

Prophetic singing develops gradually as we ascend in worship, and it cannot be rushed. It will take quality time in worship for these songs to be released. *Nataph* means to "distill gradually." This form of prophecy "distills gradually." It also means a forming, developing word, like ruminating on food. This form of prophetic utterance is slow to develop and comes like the dawn. It is possible to write such inspiration down and deliver it. An example of this is found in Job: "After I had spoken, they spoke no more; my words fell gently on their ears" (Job 29:22, NIV). As he spoke, they had unfolding revelation or understanding of God's Word to them.

Prophetic worship is a weapon of warfare because it flows out of the manifest presence of God. Where the spirit of the Lord is, there is liberty. This high form of Spirit-inspired worship brings edification, refreshing, and encouragement to the spirit. When the prophetic word of the Lord is released in song, bondages are broken, bonds are loosed, and healing and deliverance can take place. Demonic powers that have been around too long can be dispelled and cut off.[1]

Chapter 9

ACTIVATIONS THAT INVOLVE MOVEMENT AND DEMONSTRATION

THESE ACTIVATIONS INVOLVE movement and demonstration. Prophetic people can use movement. An example of this is when Elisha told the king to take arrows and smite the ground, before he released a prophetic word. In this prophetic demonstration the prophet Elisha used movement and action to show the king what it would take for him to see victory over his enemy:

> Now Elisha had become sick with the illness of which he would die. So Joash the king of Israel went down to him and wept before him, and said, "My father, my father, the chariot of Israel and its horsemen."
>
> Elisha said to him, "Take a bow and arrows." So he took a bow and arrows. Then he said to the king of Israel, "Draw the bow." So he drew it. Elisha put his hands on the king's hands.
>
> Then he said, "Open the east window." So he opened it. Then Elisha said, "Shoot." So he shot. Then he said, "The arrow of the deliverance of the LORD, and the arrow of deliverance from Aram; for *you must strike Aram in Aphek until you have destroyed them.*"
>
> Then he said, "Take the arrows." So he took them.

Then he said to the king of Israel, "Strike the ground." So he struck it three times and stood there. Then the man of God was angry with him and said, "You should have struck it five or six times. Then you would have stricken Aram until you had finished them. Now you will strike Aram just three times."

—2 KINGS 13:14–19, EMPHASIS ADDED

The activations in this chapter will help the prophetic minister to be sensitive to inspired movements that God sometimes uses in demonstrating a prophetic word. We have seen prophets use all kinds of movements in delivering the word with powerful results.

Prophetic activation #81: stomp the feet

Stomping the feet can symbolize crushing the enemy, putting your foot down, and the like. Have the person you are ministering to stomp their feet, and then launch into the prophetic flow.

Prophetic activation #82: lift the hands

Lifting the hands can represent worship, surrender to God, or the Lord lifting us. Lift the person's hands, receive a word, and launch into the prophetic flow.

Prophetic activation #83: turnaround

Turn the person around, receive a word, and launch into the prophetic flow. Words of turnaround are powerful in causing a person to see divine turnaround.

Prophetic activation #84: one step forward

Have the person you are ministering to take one step forward. Then receive a word and launch into the prophetic flow. This can represent stepping out of old things, moving forward, stepping into new realms, and so on.

Prophetic activation #85: open the hands

Have the person open his/her hands. Then receive a word and launch into the prophetic flow. Open hands can symbolize receiving from God, opening up to God, releasing your gifts, and so on.

Prophetic activation #86: pouring

Put your hands above the person's head and move as if you are pouring something on their head; then receive a word and launch into the prophetic flow. This can represent outpour, new oil, and new water coming upon the person, or the Lord filling them up.

Prophetic activation #87: loosing the hands

Have the person put his/her hands together and then loose them quickly. Receive a word and launch into the prophetic flow. This can symbolize God loosing the hands for ministry, finances, healing, and so on.

Prophetic activation #88: hand on shoulder

Place your hand on the person's shoulder, receive a word, and launch into the prophetic flow. The shoulders represent caring a burden, a ministry, a responsibility, and the like.

Prophetic activation #89: crown the person

Symbolically place a crown on the person's head, receive a word, and launch into the prophetic flow. God can crown people with glory, honor, authority, favor, and the like.

Prophetic activation #90: circle the person

Walk around the person, receive a word, and launch into the prophetic flow. Circling a person can represent protection, presence, walls coming down, and the like.

Chapter 10

ACTIVATIONS PROMPTED BY COMMON OBJECTS

THESE ACTIVATIONS USE objects that are common in prophetic churches, such as dance teams, to help inspire the prophetic minister. There are many objects you can use.

Prophetic activation #91: use a fan

Use a fan or a piece of paper to fan the person, receive a word, and launch into the prophetic flow. Fans produce wind and can represent stirring, kindling, refreshing, breath, or wind.

Prophetic activation #92: anoint with oil

Anoint the person with oil, receive a word, and launch into the prophetic flow. You can anoint the forehead (thinking), ears (hearing), throat (speaking, singing), hands (ministering), or feet (traveling, walking). These words often release a new anointing or stir up the anointing upon the recipient.

Prophetic activation #93: use a sword

Place a sword in the person's hand, receive a word, and launch into the prophetic flow. The sword represents battle, authority, angelic intervention, or cutting.

Prophetic activation #94: use a shofar

Place a shofar in the hand of the person, receive a word, and launch into the prophetic flow. A shofar is a trumpet, representing gathering, warning, calling, warfare, victory, and the like.

Prophetic activation #95: use a tambourine

Place a tambourine in the hand of the person, receive a prophetic word, and launch into the prophetic flow. The tambourine represents praise, celebration, or victory.

Prophetic activation #96: use a banner or flag

Place a small banner or flag in the hand of the person, receive a word, and launch into the prophetic flow. Flags and banners represent armies, victory, and the Lord Our Banner (Jehovah Nissi).

Prophetic activation #97: use a mantle

A mantle is a cloak that was worn by the prophets. Use a coat or cloth and place it on the person's shoulders, receive a word, and launch into the prophetic flow. Mantles represent anointings, callings, coverings, or spiritual garments.

Prophetic activation #98: use a badge

A badge represents authority. Place the badge in the person's hand, receive a word, and launch into the prophetic flow. Badges can also represent rank, access, or power.

Prophetic activation #99: use fruit

Fruit can represent character, sweetness, and prosperity. Put the fruit in the hand of the person, receive a word, and launch into the prophetic flow.

Prophetic activation #100: use a candle

Use a candle (don't light it!), put it in the person's hand, receive a word, and launch into the prophetic flow. Candles represent light, illumination, and the spirit of a man.

Chapter 11

ACTIVATIONS PROMPTED BY FOUNDATIONAL SCRIPTURE PASSAGES

T HESE ACTIVATIONS USE scriptures that are highly prophetic as a foundation for ministering to others. The prophetic minister will benefit from these activations by being sensitive to using Scripture as a means to launch into the prophetic flow.

Prophetic activation #101: Psalm 23

The LORD is my shepherd; I shall not want.
    He makes me lie down in green pastures;
He leads me beside still waters.
    He restores my soul;
He leads me in paths of righteousness
    for His name's sake.
Even though I walk
    through the valley of the shadow of death,
I will fear no evil;
    for You are with me;
Your rod and Your staff,
    they comfort me.
You prepare a table before me
    in the presence of my enemies;
You anoint my head with oil;

> my cup runs over.
> Surely goodness and mercy shall follow me
>   all the days of my life,
> and I will dwell in the house of the LORD
>   forever.

Allow the Holy Spirit to illuminate a portion of this psalm to speak to the person. There are fourteen points in this psalm you can launch from. They are:

1. The shepherd
2. No lack
3. Green pastures, which represent a place of feeding or prosperity
4. Lying down, rest
5. Restoration
6. Path of righteousness
7. No fear
8. Comfort
9. Overcoming your enemies
10. A fresh anointing or being anointed
11. Overflow
12. Goodness
13. Mercy
14. House of the Lord

Which of these points does the Holy Spirit highlight to you? Psalm 23 is the most recognizable psalm in scripture, and this psalm has ministered to most people at one time or another. Read the psalm, and launch into the prophetic flow. This activation helps the prophetic minister to launch from Scripture.

Prophetic activation #102: Psalm 27

This activation is taken from Psalm 27:1–6:

> The LORD is my light and my salvation;
>   whom will I fear?
> The LORD is the strength of my life;
>   of whom will I be afraid?
> When the wicked came against me
>   to eat my flesh—
> my enemies and my foes—
>   they stumbled and fell.
> Though an army should encamp against me,
>   my heart will not fear;
> though war should rise against me,
>   in this will I be confident.
> One thing I have asked from the LORD,
>   that will I seek after—
>   for me to dwell in the house of the LORD
>   all the days of my life,
>   to see the beauty of the LORD,
>   and to inquire in His temple.
> For in the time of trouble
>   He will hide me in His pavilion;
> in the shelter of His tabernacle He will hide me;
>   He will set me up on a rock.

Now my head will be lifted up
   above my enemies encircling me;
therefore I will offer sacrifices of joy in His tabernacle;
   I will sing, yes, I will sing praises to the LORD.

There are at least thirteen points in this psalm you can launch from. They are:

1. No fear

2. Strength

3. Overcoming your enemies

4. Confidence

5. The beauty of the Lord

6. Being hidden by God

7. Exaltation—head lifted up above your enemies

8. Mercy

9. Seeking God

10. Help

11. Being led by God

12. Faith

13. Waiting on the Lord

Which points in the psalm does the Holy Spirit highlight to you as you read this scripture over the person you are ministering to? Launch into the prophetic flow when the Holy Spirit quickens a portion of this psalm to you.

Prophetic activation #103: Isaiah 60

This activation is taken from Isaiah 60:1–5:

> Arise, shine, for your light has come,
>> and the glory of the Lord has risen upon you.
> For the darkness shall cover the earth
>> and deep darkness the peoples;
> but the Lord shall rise upon you,
>> and His glory shall be seen upon you.
> The nations shall come to your light
>> and kings to the brightness of your rising.
> Lift up your eyes all around, and see:
>> They all gather themselves together; they come
>>> to you;
> your sons shall come from afar,
>> and your daughters shall be carried at your side.
> Then you shall see and be radiant,
>> and your heart shall thrill and rejoice
> because the abundance of the sea shall be converted to
>> you,
>> the wealth of the nations shall come to you.

These scriptures highlight the glory. There are at least thirteen points in this portion of Scripture you can launch from. They are:

1. Arising
2. Shining
3. The glory of the Lord
4. Overcoming darkness

5. People attracted to the light in your life
6. Leaders coming
7. Sons and daughters coming, people gathering to you
8. Enlargement
9. Abundance
10. Conversion
11. Wealth
12. Nations coming
13. Joy

Which point does the Holy Spirit highlight? Read the verses over the person, and launch into the prophetic flow.

Prophetic activation #104: Psalm 29

This activation is taken from Psalm 29:3–9:

> The voice of the LORD is over the waters;
>> the God of glory thunders;
>> the LORD is over many waters.
> The voice of the LORD sounds with strength;
>> the voice of the LORD—with majesty.
> The voice of the LORD breaks the cedars;
>> the LORD breaks the cedars of Lebanon.
> He makes them skip like a calf,
>> Lebanon and Sirion like a wild ox.
> The voice of the LORD flashes
>> like flames of fire.
> The voice of the LORD shakes the wilderness;

the LORD shakes the Wilderness of Kadesh.
The voice of the LORD makes the deer to give birth,
 and strips the forests bare;
and in His temple everyone says, "Glory!

This passage emphasizes the voice of the Lord. Read the passage over the person you are ministering to, and launch into the prophetic flow. Be sensitive to the points the Holy Spirit highlights to you.

Prophetic activation #105: Joel 3

This activation is taken from Joel 3:18:

And it will be that in that day the mountains will drip
 sweet wine,
 and the hills will flow with milk,
 and all the streambeds of Judah will flow with
 water;
a spring will proceed from the house of the LORD
 and will water the Valley of Shittim.

This verse is chosen because it's rich in prophetic imagery. There are at least six points you can launch from. They are:

1. New wine

2. Milk, which represents prosperity

3. Rivers of Judah, praise

4. Water or refreshing

5. Fountain, life

6. Water in dry places

Read the verse over the person you are ministering to, and launch into the prophetic flow. Be sensitive to the points the Holy Spirit highlights. This activation will help the prophetic minister use Scripture, which is rich in symbolism.

Prophetic activation #106: the river of God—Psalm 46:4–5; John 7:37–38

Using a theme that is common in prophetic ministry, this activation is based on the river of God. Read these verses over the person you are ministering to, allow the Holy Spirit to highlight what portion, and then launch into the prophetic flow.

> There is a river whose streams make glad the city of God, the holy dwelling place of the Most High. God is in the midst of her; she will not be moved; God will help her in the early dawn.
>
> —PSALM 46:4–5

> On the last and greatest day of the feast, Jesus stood and cried out, "If anyone is thirsty, let him come to Me and drink. He who believes in Me, as the Scripture has said, out of his heart shall flow rivers of living water.
>
> —JOHN 7:37–38

Prophetic activation #107: dry bones—Ezekiel 37:1–10

This activation emphasizes the life-giving aspect of the prophetic anointing and another common prophetic theme of dry bones coming to life. Read the verses over the person, allow the Lord to highlight some point, and launch into the prophetic flow.

> The hand of the LORD was upon me, and He carried me out in the Spirit of the LORD and set me down in the midst of the valley which was full of bones, and He caused me to pass among them all around. And there were very many in the open valley. And they were very dry. He said to me, "Son of man, can these bones live?"
>
> And I answered, "O Lord GOD, You know."
>
> Again He said to me, "Prophesy over these bones and say to them, O dry bones, hear the word of the LORD. Thus says the Lord GOD to these bones: I will cause breath to enter you so that you live. And I will lay sinews upon you and will grow back flesh upon you and cover you with skin and put breath in you so that you live. Then you shall know that I am the LORD."
>
> So I prophesied as I was commanded. And as I prophesied, there was a noise and a shaking. And the bones came together, bone to its bone. When I looked, the sinews and the flesh grew upon them, and the skin covered them. But there was no breath in them.
>
> Then He said to me, "Prophesy to the wind; prophesy, son of man, and say to the wind: Thus says the Lord GOD: Come from the four winds, O breath, and breathe upon these slain so that they live." So I prophesied as He commanded me, and the breath came into them, and they lived and stood up upon their feet, an exceeding great army.
>
> —EZEKIEL 37:1–10

Prophetic activation #108: new thing—Isaiah 42:9; 43:19; 48:6

This activation is based on "new thing" scriptures in Isaiah. Prophecy releases new things. Read these verses over the person you are ministering to, allow the Holy Spirit to highlight one of the points, and then launch into the prophetic flow.

> See, the former things have come to pass, and new things I declare; before they spring forth I tell you of them.
> —ISAIAH 42:9

> See, I will do a new thing, now it shall spring forth; shall you not be aware of it? I will even make a way in the wilderness, and rivers in the desert.
> —ISAIAH 43:19

> You have heard; see all this. And will you not declare it? I have shown you new things from this time, even hidden things, and you did not know them.
> —ISAIAH 48:6

Prophetic activation #109: the eagle—Exodus 19:4; Psalm 103:5; Isaiah 40:31

This activation uses eagle scriptures to launch. The eagle is a symbol of the prophetic anointing, and the Lord uses this creature often in prophetic utterances. Read the verses over the person you are ministering to, allow the Lord to give you a word, and launch into the prophetic flow. This activation helps the prophetic minister to be sensitive to the symbols of creatures used in the prophetic flow.

You have seen what I did to the Egyptians, and how I lifted you up on eagles' wings, and brought you to Myself.

—Exodus 19:4

Who satisfies your mouth with good things, so that your youth is renewed like the eagle's.

—Psalm 103:5

But those who wait upon the LORD shall renew their strength; they shall mount up with wings as eagles, they shall run and not be weary, and they shall walk and not faint.

—Isaiah 40:31

Prophetic activation #110: the lion—Genesis 49:9; Proverbs 28:1; 30:30; Amos 3:8; Hebrews 11:33

This activation is based on scriptures with the word *lion*. The lion is another symbol that is often used in prophetic utterances. Read the scriptures over the person, allow the Holy Spirit to highlight one of the points, and then launch into the prophetic flow.

Judah is a lion's cub; from the prey, my son, you have gone up. He crouches and lies down like a lion; and as a lion, who dares rouse him?

—Genesis 49:9

The wicked flee when no man pursues, but the righteous are bold as a lion.

—Proverbs 28:1

...a lion which is strongest among beasts, and does not turn away for any...

—PROVERBS 30:30

The lion has roared; who will not fear? The Lord GOD has spoken; who can but prophesy?

—AMOS 3:8

Who through faith subdued kingdoms, administered justice, obtained promises, stopped the mouths of lions.

—HEBREWS 11:33

FAITH ACTIVATIONS BASED ON THE WORD

I call these faith activations because they use scriptures on faith to launch into the prophetic flow. Faith is such an important part of the believer's life that God often speaks to us in this area, and prophetic ministers often challenge people in the area of faith through the prophetic word. These activations use a portion of faith scriptures as diving boards to get into the prophetic flow.

Prophetic activation #111: Luke 1:37

For with God nothing will be impossible.

Speak this word over the recipient, and launch into the prophetic flow. Many prophecies call people to believe for the impossible. This activation will sharpen the prophetic minister's sensitivity to the importance of faith when prophesying.

Prophetic activation #112: Matthew 17:20

If you have...faith as a grain of mustard seed...

What a powerful word from the mouth of Jesus. Speak this over the recipient, and launch into the prophetic flow. There are an infinite number of words that can be given in the context of this scripture.

Prophetic activation #113: Mark 11:22

Have faith in God.

This is another activation that challenges the recipient in the area of faith. Speak these words over the recipient, and launch into the prophetic flow. Prophecy can encourage people to believe for miracles and great breakthroughs.

Prophetic activation #114: Mark 9:23

All things are possible to him who believes.

Speak this word over the recipient, receive a word, and launch into the prophetic flow. The prophetic word can move people into the realm of possibility.

Prophetic activation #115: 2 Corinthians 5:7

For we walk by faith, not by sight.

Speak this word over the recipient, receive a word, and step into the prophetic flow. This is another activation that tunes the prophetic minister's ears to hear and release words about faith and believing.

Chapter 12

CORPORATE MINISTRY ACTIVATIONS

THESE GROUP ACTIVATIONS will stretch you to be able to minster to more than one person. They will help increase your flow and your faith. Requiring flexibility and spontaneity, they show how to switch and change from ministering to one person and then move on quickly to the next person with a fresh word specifically for them. This group of activations increases faith because the prophet will have to receive a word for more than one person. These activations won't leave you much time to think or have your mind interfere with what's happening in the Spirit.

Prophetic activation #116: around the circle

Form a circle of about three to seven people. The team leader selects a person who will prophesy to the circle member directly to his/her left or right. The person who receives ministry then ministers to the person on his/her other side. This chainlike ministry continues all the way around the circle. This activation requires everyone in the circle to minister, and everyone receives a word.

Prophetic activation #117: all on one

Each person in the circle takes a turn in ministering to one circle member. The result will be an in-depth ministry to a single person. This activation demonstrates the flow of prophetic ministry and activates the prophetic minister to operate with a team.

Prophetic activation #118: one on all

This activation is designed to "stretch" a minister past his/her usual limitations. The minister is required to prophesy to each member of the circle. This exercise will build the minister's faith and confidence.

Prophetic activation #119: one prophetic word

A minister is required to give a single prophetic word to everyone in his/her circle. Each circle member ministers in this way. Circle members are to write down only the words that were given directly to them by the others. After everyone in the circle has ministered, each circle member is to read each of the words that were spoken and determine what the Lord is saying through all the words put together.

Prophetic activation #120: switch/change

At the command of the group leader, the person will switch/change between two people he/she is ministering to. Sometimes the change will be quick at the command of the leader, and sometimes slow. A quick change helps develop accuracy and quick concentration, and a slow change will force the prophetic ministry to go deeper and longer. The spontaneous switching of ministers will exercise the minister's ability to hold a prophetic word and the ability to minister at a moment's notice. The team leader simply says, "Switch," and the minister turns and ministers to the next person, and when "Switch" is said again, the minister returns to ministering to the first person.

Prophetic activation #121: group prophecy

A minister from the circle is chosen to give a common prophecy that pertains to all the circle members. This exercise is designed to help the minister become comfortable with ministering to whole groups of people, such as a congregation.

Prophetic activation #122: popcorn

The team leader will select a minister and up to five circle members. The prophetic minister is required to prophesy to all five within three minutes. The leader will stop the minister when time is up. The time limit and number of words to the five people may vary, but it must be completed in three minutes. This exercise helps overcome timidity and thought interference. This forces the minister to "dive in" and flow from his/her spirit when prophesying.

Prophetic activation #123: tunnel

Form two lines with circle members facing each other. Select one person to walk between the lines. As the person walks between the lines, each person will lay hands on them and prophesy. Those at the end of the line "tunnel" should listen to the words that come before their turn comes to minister and then launch into the prophetic flow when the person arrives to them.

Prophetic activation #124: one word, develop the word

In this activation the prophetic minister again gives one word to each member of the group. The members write down the word. After giving a single word to each of the members, the prophetic minister then returns to the first person and develops the word, launching into the prophetic flow from that one word. The minister continues this with each member in the group until completing the circle.

Prophetic activation #125: the blind prophet

The prophetic minister turns his/her back to the group. Each group member steps up behind the person one at a time. The prophetic minister releases a word to the person whom they are unable to see. This "stretches" the prophetic minister to prophesy by faith and not to be moved by what he or she sees (or doesn't see).

Three Keys for Prophetic Operation in the Local Assembly

1. Submissive and teachable in spirit

As they minister spiritual gifts, it is extremely important for all of the saints in the local assembly to truly maintain a submissive and teachable spirit toward their pastor and their local leadership. The pastors and other leaders have been given the responsibility to be shepherds for both the people in the body and for those who are ministering in their gifts.

Input and correction given by those in authority should be eagerly received by saints, who should desire to manifest their ministry in a way that will complement the philosophy of the local church. No prophetic team member should ever assume that he or she does not need to receive direction or correction from the pastor. (See Proverbs 12:15.)

We are all humans who are fallible and subject to error, so at some point in time while ministering, every one of us will make mistakes. Sometimes we will be aware that we have erred, but not always. Therefore it is important to decide beforehand to be open and willing to be corrected by those over us. It is equally important for those who have been set over the congregation to exercise their authority, not to shrink back from issuing rebukes if necessary.

When you make a mistake in the content or delivery of a public prophetic word, it is at these times in particular that your pastor can save your life. Remember that you are a member of a prophetic team, not a lone ranger, and that each one of us is only going to receive a partial revelation. At the same time, your pastor is responsible for the overall vision and the many functions of the local church.

Just because someone has a gift of prophecy, or even holds the office of the prophet in the local church, does not mean that the person can supersede his or her local pastor.

2. Do not go too long

A common complaint among pastors is that many people go too long when they prophesy or minister spiritual gifts in the church. Prophets deliver elaborate words—as long as whole sermons at times.

While it is true that prophesying is like preaching, in the sense that both have truth to present, it is equally true that a complicated or too lengthy presentation can be dull or can deaden the effect of that truth.

Most congregational prophecies can be given in one minute or less—two minutes at the most. Anything longer will become extremely wearisome for others, and it will be problematic for the pastor, who is responsible for the order, schedule, and flow of the service. Those who prophesy should endeavor to present any revelation as clearly and concisely as possible.

Along the same line, a person should not feel that he or she should prophesy at every single service, since this may limit others from ministering in their gifts and may even give the impression that this particular individual is trying to monopolize the prophetic or spiritual ministry of the church. Neither long-windedness nor frequency of prophesying should indicate higher giftedness in or honor for the speaker.

3. Flow with the order of the service

It should be obvious that prophecy is not appropriate during any part of the service when attention needs to be focused on something, in particular during the preaching, the announcements, or the altar call, when a prophetic word would be seen as an interruption. Normally the time to flow in the gifts of the Spirit is during the worship part of the service. During the brief lull between choruses, prophets can be ready to speak. The leaders should expect and encourage manifestations of the Spirit through prophecy at this time.

When saints minister during the right time of the service, their ministry should complement the flow of the service and not contradict and change the order of the service.

For example, if the congregation is involved in exuberant and demonstrative high praises of God, it would be inappropriate to share a word about being quiet and silent before the Lord. We believe that while God might share a key word with an individual saint that would change the order of the service, that responsibility would normally be given to the pastor and those appointed in leadership, and it therefore should be directed through them.

If a pastor is readily accessible during the worship service, you may share your revelation privately and allow that pastor to determine if the timing is right to share it. If not, do not be offended! You will have given what you feel God has shared with you, and it now will be in the hands of those whom God has appointed over the service.

SELECT PRINCIPLES OF PROPHETIC MINISTRY

Prophecy and the Word of Knowledge

THE GIFT OF the word of knowledge may be activated and begin to manifest during prophetic activations. The word of knowledge is a fact given about the person that only God can reveal. It can be a name, an event, a year, a situation, something from their past, something in their present, and so on. The word of knowledge has been described as a "spiritual pry bar" that can open up a person to the fact that what you are saying is from God. The word of knowledge is a "breaker" gift because it can break open people and situations that have been closed.

When the word of knowledge operates in the context of prophecy, it brings the prophetic word to another level. The word of knowledge is like a "twin" gift to the gift of prophecy. These two gifts operating together produce powerful breakthroughs on the behalf of the recipient and confirm that God knows the details of his/her life and situation. These gifts speak comfort and direction in time of need.

TONGUES AND PROPHECY

Speaking in tongues is one of the ways we edify (build up) ourselves. Prophecy builds up others. The more built up you are, the more you will be able to build up others. We can also pray in tongues to kick-start a prophetic word. Paul wrote: "I desire that you all speak in tongues, but even more that you prophesy" (1 Cor. 14:5). The Greek word translated "that" is *hina*. *Hina* can also be translated "in order that."[1] This means that an alternative translation for the Paul's message is: "I wish that you all spoke with tongues, but rather in order that you prophesied."

> In other words, Paul is saying that he wished they all spoke with tongues so that their tongues would lead into prophecy. This indicates that tongues can be used as an effective tool to "kick-start" a prophetic word. As you pray in tongues for someone or something, God may drop something in your spirit, a vision may come to you, a certain phrase, message or word may bubble up within you etc. which you can speak forth to bring edification, exhortation and comfort.[2]
>
> —DR. STUART PATTICO

DIFFERENT TRANSLATIONS OF THE VERSE "COVET TO PROPHESY"

Covet is a strong word. *Covet* means "to strongly desire." This is to be our attitude toward prophecy. First Corinthians 14:39 says, "Wherefore, brethren, covet to prophesy, and forbid not to speak with tongues" (KJV). I am providing this list of various translations of the same verse to reinforce the meaning. The word *covet* has sometimes been used in a negative sense, but there is a positive sense especially when it comes to the prophetic gift.

> So [to conclude], my brethren, earnestly desire and set your hearts on prophesying (on being inspired to preach and teach and to interpret God's will and purpose), and do not forbid or hinder speaking in [unknown] tongues.
>
> —AMPC

> So then, brothers and sisters, use your ambition to try to get the gift of prophecy, but don't prevent speaking in tongues.
>
> —CEB

> Wherefore, brethren, be zealous to prophesy; and forbid not to speak with tongues.
>
> —DRA

> So my brothers and sisters, continue to give your attention to prophesying. And don't stop anyone from using the gift of speaking in different languages.
>
> —ERV

> Therefore, my brothers, be eager to prophesy, and do not forbid speaking in other languages.
>
> —HCSB

> Therefore, brothers, earnestly pursue prophecy and do not forbid to speak with tongues.
>
> —JUB

So my brothers and sisters, you should truly want to prophesy. But do not stop people from using the gift of speaking in different kinds of languages.

—NCV

So, my dear brothers and sisters, passionately desire to prophesy; but don't ban the gift of speaking in unknown languages.

—THE VOICE

Therefore, brethren, love ye to prophesy, and do not ye forbid to speak in tongues.

—WYC

ENRICHED IN UTTERANCE

We can be enriched by God in power of speech and depth of knowledge. This is a manifestation of the grace of God.

By Him you are enriched in everything, in all speech and in all knowledge.

—1 CORINTHIANS 1:5

In that you have been enriched by him in so many ways, particularly in power of speech and depth of knowledge.

—1 CORINTHIANS 1:5, CJB

This includes being rich in the prophetic realm, and in spiritual gifts of utterance.

I thank God because in Christ you have been ·made rich [enriched] in every way, in all your ·speaking [or spiritual gifts of speaking] and in all your ·knowledge [or gifts of spiritual knowledge].

—1 CORINTHIANS 1:5, EXB

The Holy Spirit will enrich each one of us in all utterance. When somebody or something has been "enriched," it has had something extra added to it. The word carries the idea of wealth or abundance. Because we have been filled with the Holy Spirit, we should abound in utterance. The Holy Spirit is a free Spirit (Ps. 51:12), which means He is liberal, generous, and magnanimous (willing to share Himself with us). He pours Himself out upon us, and His life flows out from within us. Most often the outpouring of the Holy Spirit is released in an outpouring of prophecy. That is why we are urged not to quench or limit the Holy Spirit by quenching His inspiration.

Inspired utterances are anointed by the Holy Spirit. These words carry tremendous power and authority. Anointed words can bring deliverance, healing, strength, comfort, refreshing, wisdom, and direction.

Inspired utterances have a dramatic effect upon men and women. Their lives are enriched through the prophetic words that are spoken. Mere human words could not achieve such results. Inspired utterances are not the work of a man but the work of the Holy Spirit.

The Holy Spirit speaks through us, and He puts His word in our mouths.

> The Spirit of the LORD spake by me, and his word was in my tongue.
>
> —2 SAMUEL 23:2, KJV

David understood that his utterances were divinely inspired. David would even sing under inspiration while he played on his harp. With God's word on your tongue, your tongue can become an instrument of the divine. God desires to release His word by means of your tongue and mine. He has given every believer the gift of the Holy Spirit to accomplish His will.

Prophecy is the result of being filled with the Holy Spirit. Zacharias was dumb and unable to speak until his tongue was loosed through the infilling of the Holy Spirit. Then he not only spoke some words for the first time in months, but he also prophesied:

> Now his father Zacharias was filled with the Holy Spirit, and prophesied, saying…
> —LUKE 1:67, NKJV

Spirit-filled believers and churches should prophesy. By virtue of being filled up with the Holy Spirit, we should overflow. *Filled* is the Greek word *pietho*, meaning "to imbue, influence, or supply."

Spirit-filled believers should speak by the influence of the Holy Spirit because they have been imbued, influenced, and supplied with an abundance of the life of the Spirit of God.

Under the influence of the Holy Spirit we utter words that bring edification, exhortation, and comfort. There is always an abundant supply of such utterance given to us by the Holy Spirit.

DIFFERENT KINDS OF PROPHETIC UTTERANCE

There are different kinds of prophetic words for different situations. The prophetic word can deal with past, present, and future. The prophetic word is able to deal with all the issues we face in life. God has many thoughts toward us, and if we were to speak them, they cannot be numbered (Ps. 40:5). God's Word is a lamp to our feet and a light to our path (Ps. 119:105).

1. Now—a now word addresses issues that are currently happening in a person's life. This gives understanding for what a person is dealing with and helps eliminate confusion. I also call this a word in season. (See Isaiah 50:4.)

2. Confirmation—a word of confirmation establishes and strengthens, builds faith and removes doubt. An example is, "You are on the right track."

3. Future—this speaks to the next phase or stage in you life. It may map out directions or areas of preparation needed for future tasks. This can include instruction on what to do. God's words light our paths so we know where to go.

4. Past—these are words that deal with past issues, often bringing understanding and resolving things from the past. These words help launch us into our future. There are many people chained to the past, and they need to be released. Joseph understood his past was necessary for his purpose to his people.

5. New—a new word is something completely new. It may often surprise the recipient. It is usually something they were not thinking or planning (1 Cor. 2:9–10).

6. Warning—these words warn of dangers that may be ahead and what to avoid.

7. Deliverance—these words deliver people from things such as hurt, rejection, fear, and sickness. They release healing and restoration to the recipient (Ps. 107:20).

8. Revelation—these words give us insight and revelation into the plans and purpose of God for our lives (Deut. 29:29).

9. Identification—these words identify and help people understand and know who they are and what God created them to be (Judg. 6:12).

10. Correction—these words correct us and cause us to make the necessary adjustments in our lives (Prov. 3:11).

11. Commendation—God commends us when we are doing what is right. Each church in the Book of Revelation was commended and then corrected.

12. Exposure—these words expose and identify the works of sin and darkness (Heb. 4:13).

13. Conditional—these words are conditional on your obedience; for example, "If you

> will pray and seek My face, then I will
> move you into a new level of breakthrough
> and blessing."

14. Impartation—God uses these words, often
    accompanied with the laying on of hands,
    to impart gifts into our lives (1 Tim. 4:14).

These words can be spoken over individuals and congregations. We must be open and allow God to speak to us in these different ways. Each way will bring great blessing to the church.

Other kinds of words that bring great benefits to those who receive them include:

+ Words that heal
+ Words that deliver
+ Words that comfort
+ Words that edify
+ Words that exhort
+ Words that release courage
+ Words that release life
+ Words that refresh
+ Words that open new doors
+ Words that bring change
+ Words that release angels
+ Words that release glory
+ Words that release ministries
+ Words that expose the enemy

+ Words that release finances
+ Words that break drought
+ Words that cause breakthrough
+ Words that confirm
+ Words that release new things
+ Words that convict
+ Words that bring repentance
+ Words for the brokenhearted
+ Words for the bruised
+ Words for the poor
+ Words for the outcast
+ Words for the tired (weary)
+ Words for the lonely
+ Words for the ashamed
+ Words for the bitter
+ Words for families
+ Words for churches
+ Words for cities
+ Words for nations
+ Words for widows
+ Words for the unmarried
+ Words for those who are divorced
+ Words for the abandoned
+ Words for the grieving

+ Words to the fearful
+ Words to pastors
+ Words to apostles
+ Words to prophets
+ Words to evangelists
+ Words to teachers
+ Words to government leaders
+ Words that dissolve doubts
+ Words that break cycles
+ Words that break barrenness
+ Words that release strategies
+ Words that bring increase
+ Words that release vision
+ Words that impart gifts
+ Words that impart authority
+ Words that send out ministers
+ Words that tell you where to go
+ Words that tell you what to do
+ Words that warn
+ Words that move mountains
+ Words that root out
+ Words that pull down strongholds
+ Words that plant new things

Utterance in prophecy has a real lifting power and gives real light on the truth to those who hear. Prophecy is never a mind reflection, it is something far deeper than this. By means of prophecy we receive that which is the mind of the Lord; and as we receive these blessed, fresh utterances through the Spirit of the Lord the whole assembly is lifted into the realm of the spiritual. Our hearts and minds and whole bodies receive a quickening through the Spirit given word. As the Spirit brings forth prophecy we find there is healing and salvation and power in every line. For this reason it is one of the gifts that we ought to covet.[3]

—SMITH WIGGLESWORTH

QUENCH NOT THE SPIRIT; DESPISE NOT PROPHESYINGS

The following verses can be the reason why there is no prophecy or very little prophecy in many assemblies. We cannot despise or make light of prophecy if we desire to operate in it. Your attitude toward prophecy will determine whether or not you operate strongly in it.

Do not quench the Spirit. Do not despise prophecies.

—1 THESSALONIANS 5:19–20

Various translations of 1 Thessalonians 5:19–20 for deeper understanding

Do not quench (suppress or subdue) the [Holy] Spirit; do not spurn the gifts and utterances of the prophets [do not depreciate prophetic revelations nor despise inspired instruction or exhortation or warning].

—AMPC

Don't suppress the Spirit. Don't brush off Spirit-inspired messages.

—CEB

Quench not the Spirit; do not lightly esteem prophecies.

—DARBY

Don't stop the work of the Holy Spirit. Don't treat prophecy like something that is not important.

—ERV

Do not hold back the work of the Holy Spirit. Do not treat prophecy as if it were unimportant.

—NCV

Do not quench the Spirit. Do not treat prophecies with contempt.

—NIV

Never damp the fire of the Spirit, and never despise what is spoken in the name of the Lord.

—PHILLIPS

Don't suppress the Spirit, and don't stifle those who have a word from the Master.

—THE MESSAGE

Don't suppress the Spirit. Don't downplay prophecies.

—THE VOICE

Do not smother the Holy Spirit. Do not scoff at those who prophesy.

—TLB

The English word *despise* was translated from the Greek word *exoutheneo*, which means "to make of no account; despise utterly."[4] The word not only depicts contempt or hatred, but also it can mean as little as to ignore. It was translated "set at naught" three times in the New Testament: Luke 23:11; Acts 4:11; Romans 14:10. Paul's admonition in 1 Thessalonians 5:20 is to not hate, dislike, or ignore prophecy.

Peter also addresses the issue of prophetic ministry.

> If anyone speaks, let him speak as the oracles of God. If anyone serves, let him serve with the strength that God supplies, so that God in all things may be glorified through Jesus Christ, to whom be praise and dominion forever and ever. Amen.
>
> —1 PETER 4:11

When we speak as the oracles of God and minister with the ability God gives us, God is gloried. In other words, God is glorified through our ministering. People will praise and glorify God for the breakthroughs released in their lives through His words.

> Well if we were to look at the Greek word translated "prophecy" we would discover that it means "To speak on behalf of another." So the person who prophesies does so with the conviction that he is speaking on behalf of God. This is confirmed by the Apostle Peter's words in Scripture when he exhorts us to speak as "oracles of God" (1 Peter 4:10, 11). An oracle is a mouthpiece just like a lawyer is the mouthpiece of his client. The

one who speaks as the oracle of God—the person who prophesies—serves as the mouthpiece of the Lord.[5]

—Bob Mumford

We are not ministering to bring glory to ourselves, but we minister to bring glory to God. This is to be our attitude toward ministry.

PROPHETIC WORSHIP

Worship is one of the areas that will be greatly impacted when the prophetic gift is activated.

And he set the Levites at the house of the LORD with cymbals, harps, and lyres according to the commandment of David, and Gad the seer of the king, and Nathan the prophet. For the commandment came from the LORD through His prophets.

—2 CHRONICLES 29:25

Notice that Israel's worship was established by prophets. Hezekiah reestablished this worship based on the commandment of David, Gad, and Nathan. There is a strong connection between worship and prophetic ministry.

Prophets should be instrumental in worship. They should be involved as musicians, singers, seers, and dancers. David established worship on Mt. Zion with the prophetic families of Asaph, Heman, and Jeduthun (1 Chron. 25). Heman was the king's seer. The prophetic level in Israel at the time was extremely high because of the ministry of Samuel and the school of the prophets.

Music was evidently used in training emerging

prophets. Saul met a company of prophets who were playing instruments (1 Sam. 10). Elisha called for a minstrel and then began to prophesy. Music is very important in worship and also in training prophetic people.

Anointed minstrels help release the prophetic flow and keep it strong in an assembly. The secrets of God are opened upon the harp.

> I will incline mine ear to a parable: I will open my dark saying upon the harp.
>
> —PSALM 49:4, KJV

Minstrels should be Spirit-filled, skillful, and consecrated. They need to work with the singers and dancers in bringing forth the song of the Lord. We need prophet-musicians as a part of the worship team. If the members of the worship team are not prophets, they need to be activated in the prophetic anointing to some degree. Prophetic people are sensitive to the word of the Lord. The word of the Lord can be spoken or sung.

David, a worshipper, was also a prophet. He was the sweet psalmist of Israel.

> Now these be the last words of David. David the son of Jesse said, and the man who was raised up on high, the anointed of the God of Jacob, and the sweet psalmist of Israel, said, The Spirit of the LORD spake by me, and his word was in my tongue. The God of Israel said, the Rock of Israel spake to me, He that ruleth over men must be just, ruling in the fear of God.
>
> —2 SAMUEL 23:1–3, KJV

Sweet is the Hebrew word *na`iym*, which means "pleasant," "delightful," "sweet," "lovely," "agreeable," "delightful," "lovely," "beautiful (physical)," "singing," "sweetly sounding," "musical."

David was a singing prophet; he was also a musical prophet. Musical prophets bring great blessing and refreshing to the church. They should be identified and released. They are an important part of true worship. They release the word of the Lord in song.

Habakkuk released the word upon Shigionoth. Habakkuk 3:1 says, "A prayer of Habakkuk the prophet upon Shigionoth." The World English Bible translates this verse as, "A prayer of Habakkuk, the prophet, set to victorious music."

"To prophesy" simply means to speak or sing by inspiration. This is often spontaneous and comes as the anointing flows from within, or rests upon. The musician can play, pray, and sing by inspiration. We are inspired people. Inspiration is powerful when released in worship.

The first place we see the word *prophet* in the Bible is in Genesis 20:7, when it is used to describe Abraham. He is called an "inspired man," a prophet, one who speaks or sings by inspiration. Inspiration is the result of the breath of God. Moses desired that all of God's people were prophets (Num. 11:29).

SCRIPTURES THAT STRENGTHEN PROPHETIC FLOW

T HESE ARE SOME of the scriptures that prophetic ministers should be familiar with. Meditating on these verses will strengthen you as a prophetic minister. I would also encourage you to memorize them and be ready to use them when teaching on the subject of prophecy.

> Moses said to him, "Are you jealous for my sake? Oh, that all the people of the LORD were prophets, and that the LORD would put His Spirit upon them!"
>
> —NUMBERS 11:29

> And Balaam said to Balak, "I have come to you now. But am I able to speak just anything? The word God puts in my mouth is what I will speak."
>
> —NUMBERS 22:38

> And all these blessings will come on you and overtake you if you listen to the voice of the LORD your God.
>
> —DEUTERONOMY 28:2

> The secret things belong to the LORD our God, but those things which are revealed belong to us and to our children forever, so that we may keep all the words of this law.
>
> —DEUTERONOMY 29:29

The LORD came and stood, and He called as at other times, "Samuel, Samuel." Then Samuel said, "Speak, for Your servant listens."

—1 SAMUEL 3:10

Formerly in Israel, when a man went to inquire of God, thus he said, "Come, and let us go to the seer." For he that is now called a prophet was formerly called a seer.

—1 SAMUEL 9:9

After that you will come to the hill of God, where the garrison of the Philistines is. And when you come there to the city, you will meet a group of prophets coming down from the high place with a harp, a tambourine, a flute, and a lyre before them. And they will prophesy.

—1 SAMUEL 10:5

And the Spirit of the LORD will come upon you, and you will prophesy with them. And you will be turned into another man.

—1 SAMUEL 10:6

Then Saul sent messengers to take David, but when they saw the company of the prophets prophesying and Samuel taking his stand over them, the Spirit of God came upon the messengers of Saul and they also prophesied.

—1 SAMUEL 19:20

The Spirit of the LORD spoke by me, and His word was on my tongue.

—2 SAMUEL 23:2

Micaiah said, "As the LORD lives, I will speak whatever the LORD says to me."

—1 KINGS 22:14

Then David and the officers of the army also set apart for the service some of the sons of Asaph, and of Heman, and of Jeduthun, those who prophesied with lyres, harps, and cymbals. The number of those who did the work according to their service was:

From the sons of Asaph: Zakkur, Joseph, Nethaniah, and Asarelah, the sons of Asaph under the guidance of Asaph, who prophesied according to the decree of the king.

For Jeduthun, the sons of Jeduthun: Gedaliah, Zeri, Jeshaiah, Hashabiah, and Mattithiah, six, under the guidance of their father Jeduthun, who prophesied with the lyre in giving thanks and praise to the LORD.

—1 CHRONICLES 25:1–3

And when Asa heard these words of the prophecy of Azariah son of Oded the prophet, he was encouraged and removed the detestable idols from the entire land of Judah and Benjamin and from the cities that he captured in the hills of Ephraim. And he repaired the altar of the LORD that was before the vestibule of the LORD.

—2 CHRONICLES 15:8

So they rose up early in the morning and went out to the Wilderness of Tekoa. And when they went out, Jehoshaphat stood and said, "Listen to me, Judah and those dwelling in Jerusalem. Believe in the LORD your

God, and you will be supported. Believe His prophets,
and you will succeed."

—2 CHRONICLES 20:20

The rebuilding by the elders of the Jews prospered
through the prophesying of Haggai the prophet and
Zechariah the son of Iddo. And they built, and finished it, according to the decree of the God of Israel
and according to the decrees of Cyrus, Darius, and
Artaxerxes king of Persia.

—EZRA 6:14

See, my belly is like wine that has no vent; it is ready
to burst like new wineskins. I will speak, that I may be
refreshed; I will open my lips and answer.

—JOB 32:19–20

My heart is overflowing with a good thought; I am
speaking my works for the king; my tongue is the pen
of a skilled scribe.

—PSALM 45:1

I will hear what God the LORD will speak, for He will
speak peace to His people and to His saints, but let
them not turn again to folly.

—PSALM 85:8

He sent His word and healed them and delivered them
from their destruction.

—PSALM 107:20

This is my comfort in my affliction, for Your word
revives me.

—PSALM 119:50

You have been good to Your servant, O LORD, according to Your word.

—PSALM 119:65

Forever, O LORD, Your word is established in heaven.

—PSALM 119:89

How sweet are Your words to the taste of my mouth! Sweeter than honey to my mouth!

—PSALM 119:103

Your word is a lamp to my feet and a light to my path.

—PSALM 119:105

The giving of Your words gives light; it grants understanding to the simple.

—PSALM 119:130

A wholesome tongue is a tree of life, but perverseness in it crushes the spirit.

—PROVERBS 15:4

A man has joy by the answer of his mouth, and a word spoken in due season, how good it is!

—PROVERBS 15:23

Pleasant words are as a honeycomb, sweet to the soul and health to the bones.

—PROVERBS 16:24

Death and life are in the power of the tongue, and those who love it will eat its fruit.

—PROVERBS 18:21

A word fitly spoken is like apples of gold in settings of silver.

—PROVERBS 25:11

When there is no prophecy, the people cast off restraint, but as for he who guards instruction, happiness is his.

—PROVERBS 29:18, LEB

For thus the Lord has said to me: "Go, station a watchman; let him declare what he sees."

—ISAIAH 21:6

Then the watchman called: "O Lord, I stand continually on the watchtower in the daytime, and I am stationed at my guard post every night."

—ISAIAH 21:8

The Lord GOD has given me the tongue of the learned, that I may know how to sustain him who is weary with a word; He awakens me morning by morning; He awakens my ear to listen as the learned.

—ISAIAH 50:4

I have put My words in your mouth, and I have covered you in the shadow of My hand that I may plant the heavens, and lay the foundations of the earth, and say to Zion, "You are My people."

—ISAIAH 51:16

As for Me, this is My covenant with them, says the LORD: My Spirit who is upon you, and My words which I have put in your mouth shall not depart out of your mouth, nor out of the mouth of your descendants, nor out of the mouth of your descendants' descendants, says the LORD, from this time forth and forever.

—ISAIAH 59:21

But the LORD said to me, "Do not say, 'I am a youth.' For you shall go everywhere that I send you, and whatever I command you, you shall speak."

—JEREMIAH 1:7

Then the LORD put forth His hand and touched my mouth. And the LORD said to me, "Now, I have put My words in your mouth. See, I have this day set you over the nations and over the kingdoms, to root out and to pull down, to destroy and to throw down, to build and to plant."

—JEREMIAH 1:9–10

The prophet who has a dream, let him tell his dream. And he who has My word, let him speak My word faithfully. What is the chaff to the wheat? says the LORD.

—JEREMIAH 23:28

Again He said to me, "Prophesy over these bones and say to them, O dry bones, hear the word of the LORD."

—EZEKIEL 37:4

He reveals the deep and secret things; He knows what is in the darkness, and the light dwells with Him.

—DANIEL 2:22

And it will be that, afterwards, I will pour out My Spirit on all flesh; then your sons and your daughters will prophesy, your old men will dream dreams, and your young men will see visions.

—JOEL 2:28

And it will be that in that day the mountains will drip sweet wine, and the hills will flow with milk, and all the streambeds of Judah will flow with water; a spring will proceed from the house of the LORD and will water the Valley of Shittim.

—JOEL 3:18

Surely the Lord GOD does nothing without revealing His purpose to His servants the prophets.

—AMOS 3:7

The lion has roared; who will not fear? The Lord GOD has spoken; who can but prophesy?

—AMOS 3:8

I will stand at my watch and station myself on the watchtower; and I will keep watch to see what He will say to me, and what I will answer when I am reproved.

—HABAKKUK 2:1

Thus says the LORD of Hosts: Let your hands be strengthened, whoever is hearing these words in these days, from the mouth of the prophets who were there in the day that the house of the LORD of Hosts was founded, that the temple might be built.

—ZECHARIAH 8:9

Mary said, "I am the servant of the Lord. May it be unto me according to your word." Then the angel departed from her.

—LUKE 1:38

It is the Spirit who gives life. The flesh profits nothing. The words that I speak to you are spirit and are life.

—JOHN 6:63

He who believes in Me, as the Scripture has said, out of his heart shall flow rivers of living water.

—JOHN 7:38

He had four virgin daughters who prophesied.

—ACTS 21:9

We have diverse gifts according to the grace that is given to us: if prophecy, according to the proportion of faith.

—ROMANS 12:6

But God has revealed them to us by His Spirit. For the Spirit searches all things, yes, the deep things of God.

—1 CORINTHIANS 2:10

Follow after love and desire spiritual gifts, but especially that you may prophesy.

—1 CORINTHIANS 14:1

For you may all prophesy one by one, that all may learn and all may be encouraged.

—1 CORINTHIANS 14:31

Therefore, brothers, eagerly desire to prophesy, and do not forbid speaking in tongues.

—1 CORINTHIANS 14:39

Do not despise prophecies.

—1 THESSALONIANS 5:20

Do not neglect the gift that is in you, which was given to you by prophecy, with the laying on of hands by the elders.

—1 TIMOTHY 4:14

If anyone speaks, let him speak as the oracles of God.
If anyone serves, let him serve with the strength that
God supplies, so that God in all things may be glorified
through Jesus Christ, to whom be praise and dominion
forever and ever. Amen.

—1 PETER 4:11

PROVERBS 29:18—MUST HAVE VISION

Prophecy is God's vehicle of bringing discipline, hope,
life, structure, order, purpose, alignment, destiny, focus,
determination, faith, and divine guidance.[1]

—HAKEEM COLLINS

Here are different translations of Proverbs 29:18 for fur-
ther study and understanding on the value of vision:

Without guidance from God law and order disappear,
but God blesses everyone who obeys his Law.

—CEV

When prophecy shall fail, the people shall be scattered
abroad: but he that keepeth the law is blessed.

—DRA

A nation without God's guidance is a nation without
order. Happy are those who keep God's law!

—GNT

Where there is no vision, the people perish: but he that
keepeth the law, happy is he.

—KJV

When there is no prophecy, the people cast off restraint, but as for he who guards instruction, happiness is his.

—LEB

Where there is no word from God, people are uncontrolled, but those who obey what they have been taught are happy.

—NCV

If people can't see what God is doing, they stumble all over themselves; but when they attend to what he reveals, they are most blessed.

—THE MESSAGE

When prophecy faileth, the people shall be destroyed; but he that keepeth the law, is blessed (but he who obeyeth the Law, is blessed).

—WYC

DIFFERENT PROPHETIC STREAMS

Nabi, **meaning "to bubble up"**

The idea of the prophetic word of the Lord bubbling up refers to an unction from within to vocalize or flow like water. The word of the Lord bubbles up like a fountain and flows out of us like a river. *Nabi* describes one who is stirred up in Spirit. It is the most frequently used Hebrew word referring to prophetic utterance by the Hebrew writers. When the sense of "bubbling up" is applied to speaking, it becomes "to declare." Hence, a *nabi,* or a prophet, is an announcer—one who pours forth the declarations of God.[1]

> Be aware and sensitive to the fact that prophesies will often "bubble up" from within you and continue to "flow" as you speak it forth. The Hebrew word most often translated "prophesy" is *naba,* which literally means "to bubble up" (NAS Exhaustive Concordance) and to "flow forth."[2]
>
> —Dr. Stuart Pattico

Consider this, many saints have never prophesied in years, and many have never prophesied at all. Yet the scripture declares in Amos 3:8, when the Lord speaks, who can but prophesy? Meaning, who can't help but to prophesy. Who can't help but to respond accordingly, when the voice of the Good Shepherd is among us? For many, it may be the time and season to begin to prophesy in part to allow the Holy Spirit to bubble up from within them.[3]

Roeh, meaning "seer"

The Hebrew word *roeh* refers to a prophet's discernment. Prophets see *on* people and *through* people. *Roeh* also refers to the dreams a prophet sees. In the Bible prophets are called "seers."[4] They were given this name "because of the visions granted to them. It is first found in 1 Samuel 9:9. It is afterwards applied to Zadok, Gad, etc. (2 Samuel 15:27; 24:11; 1 Chronicles 9:22; 25:5; 2 Chronicles 9:29; Amos 7:12; Micah 3:7.) The 'sayings of seers' (2 Chronicles 33:18, 19) is rendered in the Revised Version 'the history of Hozai' (marg., the seers; so the LXX.)."[5]

Shamar, meaning "watchman"

Shamar means "to guard or protect." This can be applicable to prophetic intercession.

> By a prophet the LORD brought Israel up from Egypt, and by a prophet he was preserved.
>
> —HOSEA 12:13

Hosea 12:13 reveals to us one of the major functions of the prophet's ministry, preservation. Israel was delivered from Egypt through the ministry of Moses. Israel was preserved through the intercession of Moses (Num. 14:11–20).

Preserve means "to keep from harm, damage, danger, or

evil." It also means to protect or save. The word *preserved* is from the Hebrew word *shamar*. *Shamar* means "to hedge about" (as with thorns), "to guard," "to protect," "to watch," "to beware."[6] This word emphasizes the protective element of the prophet's mantle. The word *shamar* is first used in Scripture in Genesis 2:15. Adam is told to keep (*shamar*) the garden. It is also mentioned in Genesis 4:9. Cain asks God if he is his brother's keeper (*shamar*).

The preserving and guarding aspect of the prophet's ministry is needed in every local church. This is accomplished through intercession, discernment, praise, preaching, teaching, and worship. This guarding helps defend the church against error, heresy, witchcraft, carnality, perversion, legalism, sin, and deception.

Each church should develop and train the prophets who have been set in the assembly by God. A failure to do so can result in a local church suffering from many attacks that could have been averted. A revelation of the prophet's ministry is vital to the success and health of the church. A revelation of the *shamar* aspect of the prophet's ministry will help churches protect and defend the flock.

Again, *shamar* means "to guard," "to keep," and "to be a watchman." It can refer to guarding a flock or guarding the heart, the mind, a nation, or a city from outside attack or ungodly influences. It is used in reference to keeping (guarding) the gates or entries to cities. Each local church needs a prophetic guard. This is not one prophet but a company of prophets who will help guard the church from the invasion of the enemy. Churches that develop the prophetic ministry will have the advantage of being protected through the prophetic intercession and the *shamar* aspect of the prophet's ministry.

Hozeh, meaning "vision"

The Bible records prophets going into trances and receiving open visions.

> *Hozeh* also means "to see" or "to perceive" but is also used in reference to musicians. It is also used to describe a counselor or an advisor to a king. The Hebrew does not necessarily indicate that the person is a prophet, but rather an advisor—someone who has wisdom. It means "one who has insight." The translators try to indicate whether the message is spiritual. If it is spiritual, then they tend to translate *hozeh* as "prophet." If it does not give any indication of being spiritually generated, then they would render it "advisor" or "counselor."[7]

Prophétés, meaning "to foretell"

This word refers to a prophet's ability to make an accurate future prediction.

> In Greek writings, an interpreter of oracles or of other hidden things; one who, moved by the Spirit of God and hence his organ or spokesman, solemnly declares to men what he has received by inspiration, especially concerning future events, and in particular such as relate to the cause and kingdom of God and to human salvation.[8]

Nataph, meaning "to drop or "to preach"

Nataph refers to the tearing open of the heavens so that revelation may be brought forth. It is a releasing of freedom through energetic vocalized prophecies. It connotes fire or burning. *Nataph* means "to drop like rain," "to distill," "to prophesy like the rain."[9]

> My teaching will drop like the rain, my sayings will distill as the dew, as the droplets on the grass, and as the showers on the herb.
>
> —Deuteronomy 32:2

> After my words they did not speak again, and my speech settled on them like dew.
>
> —Job 29:22

> For He draws up the drops of water; they distill rain according to its mist, which the clouds drop down, and drip upon man abundantly.
>
> —Job 36:27–28

> Does the rain have a father? Or who has produced the drops of dew?
>
> —Job 38:28

> You crown the year with Your goodness, and Your paths drip abundance.
>
> —Psalm 65:11

> The earth shook; the heavens also poured down rain at the presence of God; even Sinai shook at the presence of God, the God of Israel.
>
> —Psalm 68:8

By His knowledge the depths are broken up, and the clouds drop down the dew.

—PROVERBS 3:20

Drip down, O heavens, from above, and let the clouds pour down righteousness; let the earth open up, and let them bring forth salvation, and let righteousness spring up together. I, the LORD, have created it.

—ISAIAH 45:8

Son of man, set your face toward the south, preach against the south, and prophesy against the forest land in the Negev.

—EZEKIEL 20:46

Son of man, set your face toward Jerusalem, and speak against the holy places, and prophesy against the land of Israel.

—EZEKIEL 21:2

And it will be that in that day the mountains will drip sweet wine, and the hills will flow with milk, and all the streambeds of Judah will flow with water; a spring will proceed from the house of the LORD and will water the Valley of Shittim.

—JOEL 3:18

Now therefore hear the word of the LORD: You say, "Do not prophesy against Israel, and do not preach against the house of Isaac."

—AMOS 7:16

Indeed, the days are coming, says the Lord, when the plowman will overtake the one who is reaping, and the treader of grapes the one who is sowing the seed; the mountains will drip sweet wine, and all the hills will flow with it.

—Amos 9:13

Appendix D

WOMEN AND PROPHECY

ANOTHER CONCERN I have addressed in the recent days and months is the subject of women in prophetic ministry. Yes, women can function in the office of a prophet as well as a prophetic believer. It is the Lord's desire that we all hear from Him and speak His word to bring edification to all who hear.

Some have misinterpreted 1 Corinthians 14:34, "Women should remain silent in the churches" to mean that women should not minister in the vocal gifts. However, Paul had already said in verse 31, "you can all prophesy in turn so that everyone may be instructed and encouraged." In the context Paul was also speaking about interruptions and disorder. Paul "suggests that another type of interruption should be avoided. Women (who were usually uneducated in that day) were asking questions in an improper manner and thus contributing to the confusion. They were told to hold their questions and ask their husbands at home. This should be applied to both men and women in matters that custom considers unbecoming. But Paul is in no sense trying to hinder women from prophesying, speaking in tongues, singing, or otherwise contributing to the worship. He expected

women to pray and prophesy if the Spirit gave them a
ministry (11:5)."[1]

—STANLEY M. HORTON

Women have special prophetic anointings that I
pointed out in chapter 1 of my book *Prophet, Arise!* I am
going to restate them here for your convenience and reference as you get activated in this gift and begin to teach
and activate others.

PASTORS WITH PROPHETIC WIVES

There are many pastors who have prophetic wives. Some
pastors want their wives to be first ladies who simply look
good and smile. Some pastors do not receive the gift that
God has placed in their wives and do not allow them or
release them to minister. This is shameful and needs to
stop. Don't allow religion and tradition to keep women
locked up in a box. God did not give women the Holy
Spirit to sit down, be quiet, and be stopped and ignored.
Pastors like this will end up in trouble because they reject
the gift that God has placed in their lives to help.

PROPHETIC WOMEN WILL HIT THE NAIL ON THE HEAD

This is a prophetic word God gave me for women, using
the example of Jael driving a nail through the head of
Sisera.

Then Jael the wife of Heber took a tent peg and a
hammer in her hand and went quietly to him, for he

was fast asleep and tired. She drove the tent peg into his temple, and it went down into the ground, so he died.

—JUDGES 4:21

Hit the nail on the head means to get to the precise point; do or say something exactly right; to be accurate; to hit the mark; to detect and expose (a lie, scandal, etc.). Prophetic women, get ready to "hit the nail on the head." Your prophetic utterances will "hit the mark."

THE DAUGHTERS OF ZELOPHEHAD

The daughters have an inheritance, and they have an inheritance in the prophetic ministry. Apostolic fathers release the daughters to prophesy, and they bless them.

> Then came near the daughters of Zelophehad, the son of Hepher, the son of Gilead, the son of Makir, the son of Manasseh, of the families of Manasseh the son of Joseph, and these are the names of his daughters: Mahlah, Noah, Hoglah, Milkah, and Tirzah. They stood before Moses, and before Eleazar the priest, and before the leaders and all the assembly by the door of the tent of meeting, saying, "Our father died in the wilderness, and he was not in the company of them that gathered against the LORD, in the company of Korah, but died in his own sin and had no sons. Why should the name of our father diminish from among his family, because he has no son? Give to us a possession among the brothers of our father."
>
> Moses brought their case before the LORD. The LORD spoke to Moses, saying: The daughters of Zelophehad speak right. You will certainly give them an inheritance

among their father's brothers, and you will cause the inheritance of their father to pass on to them.

—Numbers 27:1–7

Philip's Daughters

Philip had four daughters who prophesied, as we see in Acts 21:9. The Prophet Joel said the daughters would prophesy (Joel 2:28). There were a number of women in the Upper Room (Acts 1:14). The release of the Holy Spirit on the Day of Pentecost opened the door for women to be involved in the prophetic ministry in an unprecedented way. Women are now released to prophesy in numbers that are greater than ever before.

> "In the last days it shall be," says God, "that I will pour out My Spirit on all flesh; your sons and your daughters shall prophesy, your young men shall see visions, and your old men shall dream dreams."
>
> —Acts 2:17

Miriam

Miriam, the sister of Moses, was a prophetess. In Exodus 15:20 she led the women in dancing to celebrate God's victory over Pharaoh. She is also recognized as being sent along with Moses and Aaron to bring Israel out of Egypt. She therefore played a prominent role in Israel's deliverance from bondage.

For I have brought you up from the land of Egypt, and
from the house of slaves I have redeemed you; and I sent
before you Moses, Aaron, and Miriam.

—Micah 6:4

Huldah

Huldah was a prophetess who was recognized by King
Josiah. When the king discovered the Book of the Law,
he rent his clothes and sent men to Huldah to inquire of
the Lord. Huldah was the keeper of the king's wardrobe
and spoke the word of the Lord to the king about the
coming judgment upon Israel.

Then the king ordered…"Go and seek the Lord on my
behalf and on the behalf of the remnant in Israel and
Judah concerning what is written in the book that was
found, for the wrath of the Lord that is poured out on
us is great because our fathers have not kept the word of
the Lord, to do everything that is written in this book."

So Hilkiah and those with the king went to Huldah
the prophetess, the wife of Shallum the son of Tokhath,
son of Hasrah, who kept the wardrobe. She lived in
Jerusalem in the Second Quarter, and they spoke to her
about this.

And she said to them, "So says the Lord God of
Israel: Speak to the man who sent you all to Me."

—2 Chronicles 34:20–23

DEBORAH

Deborah was a national prophetess and judge, and she was a mother in Israel. She was recognized throughout Israel. People came to her to settle disputes. Prophets can help settle disputes. Deborah's role as a mother represented her love and compassion for Israel. Mothers can be prophets too.

> Now Deborah, the wife of Lappidoth, was a prophetess. She judged Israel at that time.
>
> —JUDGES 4:4

> Village life ceased. It ceased until I, Deborah, arose; I arose like a mother in Israel.
>
> —JUDGES 5:7

ISAIAH'S WIFE

The Prophet Isaiah considered his wife to be a prophetess. This shows that both husband and wife can be prophets. This will make a strong prophetic team.

> So I went in to the prophetess, and she conceived and bore a son. Then the LORD said to me, Call his name Maher-Shalal-Hash-Baz.
>
> —ISAIAH 8:3

ANNA

Anna was a praying and fasting prophetess. She spoke to all those who were looking for redemption and the coming Messiah. By her prayer and fasting she helped prepare the way for the Lord to come. She prayed and fasted in the temple and did not depart from the house of God. Anna is a picture of the intercessory prophet.

> And there was Anna a prophetess, a daughter of Phanuel, of the tribe of Asher. She was of a great age and had lived with her husband seven years from her virginity. And she was a widow of about eighty-four years of age who did not depart from the temple, but served God with fasting and prayer night and day. Coming at that moment she gave thanks to the Lord and spoke of Him to all those who looked for the redemption of Jerusalem.
>
> —Luke 2:36–38

PRAYERS TO ACTIVATE PROPHETIC FLOW

Reveal the things that belong to me (Deut. 29:29).

Let Your Word be revealed unto me (1 Sam. 3:7).

I bind and cast out any spirit of Absalom that would try to steal my heart from God's ordained leadership (2 Sam. 15:6).

Let Your candle shine upon my head (Job 29:3).

Lord, let Your secret be upon my tabernacle (Job 29:4).

Lead me, and make Your way straight before my eyes (Ps. 5:8).

Let my reins instruct me in the night season, and let me awaken with revelation (Ps. 16:7).

Lord, light my candle and enlighten my darkness (Ps. 18:28).

Let my eyes be enlightened with Your Word (Ps. 19:8).

Lord, cleanse my life from secret faults (Ps. 19:12).

Lead me in a plain path because of my enemies (Ps. 27:11).

Lead me and guide me for Your name's sake (Ps. 31:3).

Guide me with Your eye (Ps. 32:8).

Send out Your light and truth, and let them lead me (Ps. 43:3).

Open Your dark sayings upon the harp (Ps. 49:4).

Guide me by the skillfulness of Your hands (Ps. 78:72).

Let me understand Your deep thoughts (Ps. 92:5).

Let me guide my affairs with discretion (Ps. 112:5).

Open my eyes to behold wondrous things out of Your Word (Ps. 119:18).

Hide not Your commandments from me (Ps. 119:19).

Let me understand and have revelation of Your will and purpose (Ps. 119:130).

I reject the mouth of vanity and the right hand of falsehood (Ps. 144:8).

Let me understand Your parables, the words of the wise and their dark sayings (Prov. 1:6).

My spirit is the candle of the Lord, searching all the inward parts of the belly (Prov. 20:27).

Make the crooked places straight and the rough places smooth before me (Isa. 40:4).

Let Your glory be revealed in my life (Isa. 40:5).

Make darkness light before me and crooked things straight (Isa. 42:16).

Give me the treasures of darkness and hidden riches in secret places (Isa. 45:3).

Let Your righteousness be revealed in my life (Isa. 56:1).

Guide me continually (Isa. 58:11).

Lord, give me strength to bring forth my destiny as Your prophet (Isa. 66:9).

I reject every false vision and every false prophetic word released into my life (Jer. 14:14).

I call to You, and You will answer me and show me great and mighty things that I do not know (Jer. 33:3).

Reveal to me the secret and deep things (Dan. 2:22).

You are a God that reveals secrets. Lord, reveal Your secrets unto me (Dan. 2:28).

Let me have and walk in an excellent spirit (Dan. 6:3).

Let the seals be broken from Your Word (Dan. 12:9).

Reveal Your secrets to Your servants the prophets (Amos 3:7).

Lord, stir up my spirit to do Your will (Hag. 1:14).

Lead me not into temptation, but deliver me from evil (Matt. 6:13).

Hide Your truths from the wise and prudent, and reveal them to babes (Matt. 11:25).

Let me understand things kept secret from the foundation of the world (Matt. 13:35).

Lord, let no man deceive me (Matt. 24:4).

Let me know and understand the mysteries of the kingdom (Mark 4:11).

Let the hidden things be made manifest (Mark 4:22).

Lord, let me not operate in the wrong spirit (Luke 9:55).

My eyes are blessed to see (Luke 10:23).

Let me understand heavenly things (John 3:12).

Let Your arm be revealed in my life (John 12:38).

Guide me into all truth (John 16:13).

Let all spiritual cataracts and scales be removed from my eyes (Acts 9:18).

Let me speak the wisdom of God in a mystery (1 Cor. 2:7).

Let me understand the deep things of God (1 Cor. 2:10).

I bind and cast out all spirits of self-deception in the name of Jesus (1 Cor. 3:18).

Let me be a good steward of Your revelations (1 Cor. 4:1).

Let me speak to others by revelation (1 Cor. 14:6).

Let me receive visions and revelations of the Lord (2 Cor. 12:1).

Let me receive an abundance of revelations (2 Cor. 12:7).

I bind and rebuke any bewitchment that would keep me from obeying the truth (Gal. 3:1).

Make known unto me the mystery of Your will (Eph. 1:9).

Give me the spirit of wisdom and revelation, and let the eyes of my understanding be enlightened (Eph. 1:17–18).

Let me comprehend with all saints what is the breadth, length, depth, and height of Your love (Eph. 3:18).

Let me make known the mystery of the gospel (Eph. 6:19).

Let me speak the mystery of Christ (Col. 4:3).

Lord, give me wisdom in every area where I lack it (James 1:5).

I reject all false prophetic ministry in the name of Jesus (2 Pet. 2:1).

I bind Satan, the deceiver, from releasing any deception into my life (Rev. 12:9).

I bind and cast out any spirit of sorcery that would deceive me in the name of Jesus (Rev. 18:23).

PROPHETIC WORDS AND SYMBOLS

ELOW ARE WORDS and names that are often used in prophecy. It would be good for prophetic people to be familiar with prophetic language, or language of the Spirit. It is good to expand your prophetic vocabulary in order to better articulate what the Lord is showing you.

A

Aaron—priest, ministry, shepherd (Ps. 77:20)

Abigail—wisdom and grace (1 Sam. 25:3)

Abraham—the father of the faithful, pioneer, and spiritual legacy (Rom. 4:12)

Absalom—rebellion and vanity (2 Sam. 14:25)

Agabus—new covenant prophet found in the Book of Acts (Acts 11:28; 21:10–11)

age—a generation, a long period of time (Eph. 2:7; 3:5); the kingdom age is the "age of ages"

alabaster box—worship, perfume vase, fragrance of Jesus Christ's sacrifice and brokenness (Matt. 26:7; Mark 14:3; Luke 7:37)

alarm—warning, blowing the trumpet (Joel 2:1)

altar—place of sacrifice, worship, repentance (Ps. 43:4)

Amos—a prophet raised up by God outside of the prophetic community (Amos 7:14)

angel—messenger, protector (Ps. 103:20)

angel of light—a description of Satan, who appears to be righteous in order to deceive; also, false ministers (2 Cor. 11:14)

ant—diligence, preparation (Prov. 6:6–8)

Antioch—ministering to the Lord, apostolic release (Acts 13:1–3)

apostle—sent one, ambassador, commissioner of Christ (1 Cor. 12:28)

Aquila and Priscilla—team ministry, apostolic teams, upgrade (Acts 18:26)

ark—place of salvation and safety, place of God's glory (1 Pet. 3:20)

Asaph—musical prophet, worship (1 Chron. 16:37)

B

Babel—rebellion, pride, confusion (Gen. 11:9)

Babylon—defeat, mourning, captivity, and bondage (Ps. 137:1)

Balaam—soothsayer, divination, stumbling block (Josh. 13:22)

balm—healing and restoration (Jer. 8:22)

banner/ensign—a flag representing gathering, victory (Ps. 20:5)

Barnabas—encourager, comforter, divine connections (Acts 4:36) Bashan—proud and lofty (Isa. 2:13)

beast—cruel, vicious, strong (Dan. 7)

beautiful feet—preaching the gospel (Rom. 10:15)

Belial—wicked and worthless; wicked men (Deut. 13:13)

belly—innermost being, spirit (John 7:38)

Berean—noble, studious (Acts 17:11)

Bethany—the place where the Lord rested, a place of welcome, hospitality (Matt. 21:17)

Bethesda—healing, miracles (John 5:2–3)

Bethel—house of El, or house of God; the place of God's presence; the gateway of heaven (Gen. 28:11–19)

Bethlehem—house of bread, the place of birthing and provision, the city of David

birth/birthing—to bring forth, initiate, begin (Isa. 66:9)

black—moral darkness, sin, apostasy; or hidden, mysterious

blue—the heavens, heavenly places

book—the Word, learning, education, teaching

brass—cleansing, purging, judgment, strength (Rev. 1:15)

break/breaker—break out, break open, break forth (Jer. 23:29)

breath—spirit, life, vitality, Holy Spirit, prophecy (John 20:22)

burden—a weight, the weight of the prophetic word, what the prophet carries; prophecy was often referred to as "a burden" (Nah. 1:1)

butter—richness, prosperity, depth of the Word, discernment (Isa. 7:22)

C

Caleb—another spirit, faith, possessing the land (Num. 14:24)

Carmel—excellency, glory (Isa. 35:2)

Canaan—inheritance, possession, promised land (Ps. 105:11)

candle—light, direction, spirit of man, revelation (Matt. 5:15)

Cave of Adullum—a hiding place; the place of training, healing, and restoration (1 Sam. 22:1)

charge—order, command (1 Tim. 1:18)

chariot—battle, riding into battle, victory, angelic host (Ps. 68:17)

cloud by day, fire by night—divine protection and guidance (Exod. 13:21)

comfort—soothe, give solace, give rest (1 Cor. 14:3)

commission—to send out with full power and authority; an assignment, mandate company of the prophets—a prophetic community, gathering of prophets in different locations (1 Sam. 19:20)

covenant—agreement and union between individuals and between God and men (Gen. 15:18)

cover/covering—protect, hide, under authority (Ps. 91:4)

create—form, make something new (Ps. 51:10)

crown—authority, favor, rule, honor (Ps. 8:5)

cup—salvation, drinking, filling, vessel, overflow; can also represent judgment (Ps. 116:13)

curtain—veil, separation

Cyrus—apostolic decree, shepherd, treasures of darkness, hidden wealth (Isa. 45:1–3)

D

Daniel—excellent spirit, visionary, intercessor (Dan. 6:3)

dark saying—hidden or mysterious; a parable (Ps. 49:4)

darkness—blindness, ignorance, sorrow, distress, hidden, obscure, ignorance, not revealed (John 8:12)

David—king, prophet, worshipper, champion, shepherd, a man after God's heart (1 Sam. 13:14)

decree—an authoritative word released by someone in authority that becomes law (Job 22:28)

deep/depths—hidden things, beneath the surface (Dan. 2:22)

diamond—splendor, beauty, value (Exod. 28:18)

discern—to see clearly, to see the motives, differentiate, separate (Mal. 3:18)

deliver—rescue, redeem, save, set free (2 Tim. 4:17)

dew—refreshing, blessing, prosperity (Gen. 27:28)

dove—Holy Spirit, gentleness, beloved, innocence (Matt. 3:16) double portion—that which belongs to the firstborn, inheritance (2 Kings 2:9)

drama—to act out, demonstrate; sometimes the prophetic word is dramatized or acted out by the prophet (Acts 21:11)

E

eagle—sharpness, sight, vision, height, a picture of the prophetic anointing; an eagle can also be symbolic of an evil spirit depending on the context of the dream (Isa. 40:31)

earthquake—a shaking, judgment, shaking the foundation (Ps. 82:5)

Ebenezer—stone of help, divine help and assistance (1 Sam. 7:12)

Eden—the garden of God, the place of fruitfulness and restoration (Isa. 51:3)

Egypt—the place of slavery, bondage, and captivity; the old world; also a place of sustenance and transition (Exod. 13:3)

Eldad and Medad—prophesying outside the tabernacle (Num. 11:26)

Eli—spiritual blindness (1 Sam. 4:15)

Elijah—intercession, the prophetic ministry, judgment, prophetic father (1 Kings 17:1)

Elim—a place of refreshing, an oasis (Num. 33:9)

Elisha—double portion, impartation, prophetic father (2 Kings 2:9)

Enoch—walking with God (Gen. 5:22)

ephod—priesthood ministry (Heb. 4:14)

Esau—the flesh and carnality (Heb. 12:16)

Esther—favor, scepter, deliverance, divine providence (Esther 2:17)

Ezekiel—visionary prophet, judgment (Ezek. 1:1)

F

favor—blessing, advantage (Ps. 106:4)

fire—purging, judgment, passion, zeal (Ps. 104:4)

flies—Beelzebub, uncleanness, evil spirits (Eccles. 10:1)

flint—strength and hardness in the midst of opposition (Isa. 50:7)

fountain—a flow of water, refreshing, life, and blessing (Joel 3:18)

fox—crafty, sly, political (Luke 13:32)

fresh anointing—new anointing, new ability, new power (Ps. 92:10)

friend of God—prophets, understanding God's secrets (James 2:23)

frog—unclean spirit (Rev. 16:13)

furnace—a place of affliction, trouble, testing (Deut. 4:20)

G

garment—a covering, authority, identity

gatekeeper—a spiritual guard, sentry; authority to guard and protect a church, city, or region

gem—valuable, bright, brilliant, beauty

giant—a large spiritual enemy that you will need God's power to overcome (1 Sam. 17:4)

girdle—a belt or waistband representing preparedness to fulfill a duty; truth (Matt. 3:4)

goat—carnal, unbelieving (Matt. 25:32–33)

gold—purity, prosperity, holiness, royalty, something precious, refining, righteousness; glory of God; self-glorification (Prov. 17:3)

Goliath—the giant; represents arrogance and intimidation (1 Sam. 17:4)

golden calf—idol (Exod. 32:4)

Goshen—a place of safety and protection (Exod. 8:22)

grace—divine ability, endowment, favor, gifting (2 Cor. 12:9)

grass—symbolic of the green pastures of God (Ps. 23:2); withered grass is symbolic of those who do wrong (Ps. 37:2)

gray—mixture, half truth, compromise

gray hair—wisdom, a crown of glory (Prov. 16:31)

green—growth, prosperity, abundance; also envy, witchcraft, jealousy (Ps. 52:8)

H

hair—glory, covering (1 Cor. 11:15)

Hagar—slave woman; law, legalism, mockery (Gen. 21:9)

Haman—wicked plots (Esther 3)

hammer—to smash; a strong weapon (Jer. 23:29)

Hannah—birthing, intercession, travail (1 Sam. 1:20)

heart—mind, spirit, inner man (Prov. 4:23)

hedge—restrain, protection (Isa. 5:5)

honey—sweetness, blessing, abundance (Num. 14:8)

horn—power and strength (Ps. 89:17)

hornet—affliction, stinging, biting words, slander, strife, curse (because of sin), persecution, trouble, offense, demon spirits (Deut. 7:20)

horse—strength, swift, pride (Job 39:19)

hour—a present time, a time quickly approaching (John 4:23)

hunger and thirst—greatly desire (Matt. 5:6)

hyssop—purification (Heb. 9:19)

I

impart/impartation—to transfer from one person to another; a deposit (Rom. 1:11) incense—prayer, intercession, worship, sacrifice (Ps. 141:2)

iron—strength, powerful, invincible, stronghold, stubborn (Dan. 2:40)

Isaac—the son of inheritance, the blessing of the father, the next generation of promise

Isaiah—preaching prophet, restoration, glory (Isa. 6)

issue of blood—long-standing problem, infirmity (Luke 8:43)

Ishmael—born after the flesh, the work of the flesh, persecution (Gal. 4:29)

Israel—prince of God, the true people of God (Gen. 32:28)

Issachar—knowing the times and seasons (1 Chron. 12:32)

J

Jabez—breakthrough, expansion, blessing (1 Chron. 4:10)

Jacob—trickster, liar, conniver (Gen. 27:36)

Jeremiah—called from the womb, weeping prophet, young prophet (Jer. 1:5–10)

Jerusalem—city of God, place of authority, teaching, doctrine (Isa. 2:3)

Jezebel—idolatry, seduction, witchcraft, and whoredom; also a symbol of false prophets (2 Kings 9:22; Rev. 2:20)

Job—suffering, loss, restoration (Job 42:12)

Joel—outpouring of the Holy Spirit, restoration (Joel 2:28–32)

John the Baptist—calling men to repentance, holiness (Matt. 3:1)

Jonah—running away from your assignment; prophet on the run (Jon. 1:3)

Jonathan—loyalty and covenant love (1 Sam. 18:3)

Joseph—favor, dreamer, promotion, exaltation (Gen. 37:3)

Joshua—warrior, victor, possessing the land, driving out giants (Deut. 3:28)

Judah—praise; the place of liberty, praise, blessing, victory (Gen. 49:8)

Judas—betrayal, treachery, conspiracy (Mark 3:19)

justice—righteousness; righteous behavior and actions toward others; prophets are lovers of justice (Prov. 21:3)

K

key of David—power to open and close the sanctuary (Isa. 22:22)

keys—control, jurisdiction, access, authority, binding and loosing (Matt. 16:19)

king—rule, reign, authority, power (Eccles. 8:4)

kingdom of God—the rule and reign of God in and through the saints; righteousness, peace, and joy in the Holy Spirit (Rom. 14:17)

L

Laban—trickster, liar, deceiver (Gen. 31:41)

Lazarus—resurrection, life from the dead (John 11:43)

Lebanon—prosperity, glory, beauty (Isa. 35:2)

leaven—sin, corruption, hypocrisy (1 Cor. 5:8)

lifting hands—worship and adoration, praise, total surrender (Ps. 141:2; Rev. 10:5; 1 Tim. 2:8; Neh. 8:6)

lion—fierce, boldness, courage, a picture of apostolic ministry (Prov. 28:1)

Levi—the priesthood, holiness, consecration, teaching (Ps. 135:20)

Leviathan—sea monster, pride, arrogance, haughtiness, stubbornness (Job 41)

locust—devourer, poverty, lack (Joel 1:4)

Lot—wrong location, preacher of righteousness, delivered (2 Pet. 2:7)

M

manna—sustenance, Word of God (Ps. 78:24)

mantle—a cloak, a covering, an anointing, power, ability
(1 Kings 19:19)

Marah—bitterness; the place of hurt, shame, bitterness
(Exod. 15:23)

mark—a symbol of ownership; can be positive or negative (Ezek. 9:4)

Melchizedek—royal priesthood, a priest and a king, new covenant
ministry (Gen. 14:18)

milk—nourishment, growth, teaching, doctrine (Joel 3:18)

Mizpah—a watchtower, a place for proper judgment and discernment (1 Sam. 7:6)

Moses—deliverer, savior, lawgiver (Ps. 105:26)

moth—deterioration; a moth is an insect of darkness; loss through
deceit; secret or undetected trouble; corruption, chastise-
ment (Hosea 5:12)

Mount Carmel—contending with idolatry and false prophets, victory, God's power (1 Kings 18)

Mount Sinai—the law, the giving of the Word, old covenant,
bondage, legalism (Exod. 19)

mountain—a large mountain can symbolize the prosperity and favor
of God on your life (Ps. 30:6-7); a treacherous or foreboding
mountain can symbolize an obstacle or resistance; moving a
mountain can symbolize faith in God (Ps. 125:1); mountains
can also symbolize nations or life's journey (Isa. 2:2; Jer. 51:25)

midnight—intense darkness, deliverance (Exod. 11:4)

N

Nazirite—holiness, separation, consecration (Judg. 13:7)

net—evangelism; a trap, a snare (Eccles. 9:12)

new heaven/new earth—new world (age), change of ages, new covenant world (Isa. 66:22)

new name—name change, new identity, new assignment, new authority (Isa. 62:2)

Nehemiah—restoration, rebuilding the walls; comforter

number, two—witness, double

number, seven—number of completion

number, eight—number of new beginnings

number, twelve—order and apostolic authority

number, forty—a generation, temptation, testing, wilderness (Ps. 95:10)

number, fifty—jubilee, freedom, liberty, release, Pentecost (Lev. 25:10)

number, one thousand—perfection, completion (Isa. 60:22)

O

oak tree—deep roots, strength (Josh. 24:26)

oil—anointing, favor, promotion (Ps. 92:10)

Og—king of Bashan; a giant (Deut. 3:3)

olive tree—source of anointing oil, prosperity (Zech. 4:11)

open heaven—answered prayer (Deut. 28:12)

oracle—a divine message given by a deity; there were pagan oracles (Delphi was one), and there is the true oracle of the Lord (1 Pet. 4:11)

ox—strength, symbol of apostolic anointing, plowing, hard worker (Prov. 14:4)

P

palace—a place of rule, promotion, exaltation (Gen. 41:14)

palm tree—an oasis, a place of strength and growth (Ps. 92:12) parable—a short allegorical story designed to illustrate or teach some truth, religious principle, or moral lesson (Ps. 49:4)

Passover—redemption, removing sin (leaven), deliverance (Exod. 12:11)

Paul—apostle of revelation, missionary, writer, apostolic father (Eph. 3:1–9)

pearl—valuable, rare, beauty, great price, hidden (Matt. 13:46)

pen—writing, scribe (Ps. 45:1)

Pentecost—outpouring of the Holy Spirit; firstfruits (Acts 2:1)

Pharisee—religious spirit, critical, judgmental, religious pride (Matt. 5:20)

Philistine—uncircumcised, enemy of the Spirit (1 Sam. 17:26)

pillar—support, strength in the house of God (Rev. 3:12)

pit—a low place, place of captivity, hidden place (Gen. 37:24)

plow—break up the ground, open hard places (Hosea 10:11)

plumb line—standard, measurement, correction, adjustment (Amos 7:7)

priest—minister of God, intercession, offering sacrifices

prophet—an inspired man or woman, seer (1 Cor. 12:28)

purple—color of royalty (Songs 3:10)

python—a constrictor, to choke, squeeze the life out of, divination (Acts 16:16)

R

rags—poverty (Isa. 64:6)

rain—blessing, favor, abundance, refreshing (Ps. 68:9)

rainbow—covenant, mercy (Gen. 9:13)

Ramah—the place of prophetic ministry, a prophetic atmosphere, a place of training red—atonement, forgiveness, redemption; can also mean sin, corruption, harlotry (scarlet)

Red Sea—the place of transition and crossing over; the place of judgment for God's enemies (Exod. 15:3–5)

Rehoboth—a place of enlargement and flourishing (Gen. 26:22)

restore/restoration—bring back, heal, rebuild, recover (Joel 2:25)

remnant—the faithful, the true worshippers (Isa. 37:32)

repairer of the breach—to repair, restoration, to recover (Isa. 58:12)

ring—authority, signet, seal, covenant (Gen. 41:42)

River, Jordan—a place of transition or crossing over; crossing over into an inheritance (Josh. 1:2)

rivers—a flow; a place of water, life, refreshing (Isa. 33:21)

Rizpah—unconditional love (2 Sam. 21:9–11)

roar—sound of victory, lion, judgment (Amos 3:8)

rock—stability, strong foundation (Ps. 18:46)

S

sacred cow—a tradition that has become an idol

Salem—peace (Heb. 7:2)

Samuel—intercessor, prophet, training, prophetic father (1 Sam. 7:13)

salt—seasoning or preservative (Matt. 5:13)

Samson—strength, deliverance, power, judge

sand—shifting, no foundation, multiplication (Matt. 17:26)

Sarah—mother of nations (Gen. 17:15)

Satan—adversary, slanderer (Matt. 16:23)

Saul—controlling leadership, rejection by God, attacking God's anointed

scroll—God's or man's written word (Ezek. 3:1–3)

sea—peoples, nations (Ps. 72:8)

seal—a stamp, that which authenticates (1 Cor. 9:2)

season—a timeframe in which the purposes of God are fulfilled (Eccles. 3:1)

season, autumn—end, completion, change, repentance (Isa. 64:6; Jer. 8:20)

season, spring—fresh start, renewal, salvation, refreshing (Isa. 43:19; Acts 3:19)

season, summer—opportunity, harvest time, trail, affliction (Prov. 10:5)

season, winter—waiting, not friendly, death (Jer. 8:20)

seat—a place of authority, rest from your enemies (Matt. 23:2)

seducing spirit—a demon of deception (1 Tim. 4:1)

seer—ability to see, discernment, visionary, watchman; prophets were called seers (1 Sam. 9:9)

serpent—crafty, demonic, wisdom (Matt. 10:16)

scepter—a rod of authority; ruling and reigning (Gen. 49:10)

scorpion—evil spirit, pain, torment (Rev. 9:5)

shaking—removing the old, judgment, change (Isa. 37:7)

shalom—peace, prosperity, health (Isa. 26:3)

Sharon—a place of flocks, beauty (Isa. 35:2)

shield—protection, guard (Gen. 15:1)

Shiloh—peace, abundance (Gen. 49:10)

shofar—a trumpet, sounding the alarm, calling together, gathering, announcement (Josh. 6:13)

shoulder—ability to carry, burden, government, responsibility (Isa. 9:6)

showers—abundance of rain, blessings, refreshing, prosperity (Ezek. 34:26)

Siloam—an apostolic pool; a place of seeing, restoration of eyesight (John 9:7)

silver—redemption, prosperity (Prov. 25:4)

sleep—rest, slumber; could be positive or negative (Matt. 26:45)

sloth—laziness, sluggard (Prov. 19:15)

Sodom—perversion, pride (Isa. 3:9)

Solomon—wisdom, majesty, glory, peace (1 Kings 4:29)

spider—web, trap, deceit (Isa. 59:5)

staff—shepherding, protecting, comfort (Ps. 23)

strongman—a ruling spirit that controls a person or region that can only be overcome by someone stronger (Matt. 12:29)

sword—Word of God, warfare, victory, cutting (Heb. 4:12)

T

table—conference, provision, agreement, covenant (Ps. 23)

tabernacles (Feast of)—harvest, joy, God dwelling with us (Lev. 23:34)

tambourine—joy, praise (Ps. 81:2; Jer. 31:4)

tent—dwelling place, safety, covering (Isa. 54:2)

thorns—unfruitfulness, curse, pain, vexation (Gen. 3:18)

throne—place of power and rule (Ps. 122:5)

Timothy—apostolic sons and daughters (2 Tim. 1:2)

transition—to move from the old to the new

U

Urim and Thummim—stones given to the priests to obtain direction from God; the oracular aspect of the priesthood; a picture of the prophetic anointing (Deut. 33:8)

V

valley—a low place; a place of rest (Ps. 104:10)

valley of decision—a place of decision, turning point, judgment (Joel 3:14)

vineyard—the church, fruitfulness (Mark 12:2)

veil—deception, without understanding, law, hidden/concealed (Luke 24:45)

vessel—chosen, a container of the anointing (2 Tim. 2:21)

voice of the Lord—power, Word of God (Ps. 29)

vulture—death and defeat (Isa. 34:15)

W

warn/warning—to alert of danger, often impending; to warn of impending judgment (Ezek. 3:18)

watch/watchman/watchtower—place of vision, prayer, guarding, protection, ward (Isa. 21:6, 8)

web—snare; lies/deception (Eccles. 7:26)

wells—places of water, life, and refreshing (John 4:14)

wheat—harvest, abundance (Ps. 147:14)

wilderness—dry place, testing, trial, loneliness (Ps. 102:6)

windows of heaven—abundance, overflow, outpour, more than enough (Mal. 3:10)

wind—breath, change, power, blowing out, blowing in (Ps. 147:18)

wealthy place—large place, plenty, prosperity (Ps. 66:12)

weight—the glory of God is called a "weight" (2 Cor. 4:17)

whirlwind—change, God appearing, judgment (Job 40:6)

white—cleansing, purity, forgiveness (Isa. 1:18)

windows of heaven—blessing, overflow, prosperity (Mal. 3:10) wine—Holy Spirit; blessing and abundance (Joel 3:18)

wineskin, new—new churches and ministries that can contain new wine; the shape or form of ministry, container (Matt. 9:17)

wineskin, old—outmoded and outdated forms of ministry (Matt. 9:17)

wings—soaring, prophet, demon, shelter, Holy Spirit (Hosea 12:13)

wolf—greedy, voracious, vicious, false prophets (Matt. 7:15)

wolf/lamb—harmony between former enemies; Jew and Gentile joined together (Isa. 11:6; 65:25)

wrestle/wrestling—perseverance, struggle, travail (Gen. 32:24)

Y

yoke—a joining together, minister together, bondage, slavery (Phil. 3:4; Isa. 58:6)

Z

Zadok—a priest with a seer's anointing (2 Sam. 15:27)

Zarephath—the place of sustenance and provision, where Elijah was sent to the widow (1 Kings 17:9)

Zion—the hill of God; a high place; the place of the kingdom, a godly stronghold; the place of glory and reign; the city of God; the New Jerusalem (Ps. 48:2)

NOTES

Introduction
Be Released Into a Greater Prophetic Dimension

1. Tim and Theresa Early, "Apostolic Impartation and Prophetic Activation for Destiny," ReadBag.com, accessed January 6, 2016, http://www.readbag.com/apostlesandprophets -teaching-documents-pdfs-apostolic-impartation-and-prophetic -activation-for-destiny.

2. Benjamin Schäfer, "Prophetic Activation Exercises," A Yearning Hearts Journey, accessed December 19, 2015, http:// yearningheartsjourney.blogspot.com/2012/02/prophetic-activation -exercises.html.

3. Ibid.

4. Geoff and Gina Poulter, *The Gift of Prophecy for Today* (N.p.: Renata Trust, 2011).

5. Steve Thompson, *You May All Prophesy* (N.p.: Morning-Star Publications, 2007).

6. Ralph F. Wilson, "Understanding the Gift of Prophecy II: the Purpose of Prophecy Today," Joyful Heart Renewal Ministries, accessed December 19, 2015, http://www.joyfulheart.com /scholar/purp-pro.htm.

7. B. Dale, "A Company of Prophets," Biblehub.com, accessed December 11, 2014, http://biblehub.com/sermons /auth/dale/a_company_of_prophets.htm.

8. "School of the Prophets in the Bible," The Well Prophetic Institute, accessed March 30, 2015, http://www.thewellchurch .net/ministries/training-and-equipping/prophetic-institute/.

CHAPTER 1
BEGINNING ACTIVATIONS

1. This list is taken from John Eckhardt, *God Still Speaks* (Lake Mary, FL: Charisma House, 2009), 223–225.

CHAPTER 3
ACTIVATIONS PROMPTED BY THE NAMES OF GOD

1. "The Names of God in the Old Testament," BlueLetter Bible.org, accessed December 19, 2015, https://www.blueletter bible.org/study/misc/name_god.cfm.
2. Ibid.
3. Ibid.

CHAPTER 5
TEAM MINISTRY ACTIVATIONS

1. Eckhardt, *God Still Speaks*, 38–41.

CHAPTER 6
BIBLE ACTIVATIONS

1. Stefan Misaras, "We All Have to Capacity to Prophesy as We Eat, Drink, and Enjoy the Lord," *A God-Man in Christ* (blog), June 7, 2012, accessed December 19, 2015, http://www .agodman.com/blog/we-all-have-the-capacity-to-prophesy-as-we -eat-drink-and-enjoy-the-lord/.

CHAPTER 7
PROPHETIC PRAYER ACTIVATIONS

1. John Eckhardt, *Deliverance and Spiritual Warfare Manual* (Lake Mary, FL: Charisma House, 2014), 94.

CHAPTER 8
PROPHETIC SONGS AND WORSHIP ACTIVATIONS

1. Eckhardt, *Deliverance and Spiritual Warfare Manual*, 106–108.

APPENDIX A
SELECT PRINCIPLES OF PROPHETIC MINISTRY

1. Joseph H. Thayer, *Thayer's Greek-Hebrew Lexicon of the New Testament* (N.p.: Hendrickson Publishers, 1995).

2. Stuart Pattico, "How to Prophesy and Move in the Prophetic," StuartPattico.com, accessed December 19, 2015, http://www.stuartpattico.com/how-to-prophesy-and-move-in -the-prophetic.html.

3. Smith Wigglesworth, *Ever-Increasing Faith* (N.p.: Wigglesworth Books, 2013).

4. Strong's G1848, BlueLetterBible.org, accessed December 20, 2015, https://www.blueletterbible.org/lang/lexicon/lexicon .cfm?Strongs=G1848&t=KJV.

5. Bob Mumford, "Levels of Prophecy," accessed January 27, 2016, http://spirit-of-god.blogspot.com/2006/07/levels-of -prophecy-by-bob-mumford.html.

APPENDIX B
SCRIPTURES THAT STRENGTHEN PROPHETIC FLOW

1. Hakeem Collins, *Born to Prophesy* (Lake Mary, FL: Creation House, 2013), 271.

APPENDIX C
DIFFERENT PROPHETIC STREAMS

1. "Bible Verses About Prophet," *Forerunner Commentary*, BibleTools.org, accessed December 19, 2015, http://www.bible

tools.org/index.cfm/fuseaction/Topical.show/RTD/CGG/ID /5960/Prophet.htm.

2. Stuart Pattico, "How to Prophesy and Move in the Prophetic," StuartPattico.com, accessed December 19, 2015, http:// www.stuartpattico.com/how-to-prophesy-and-move-in-the -prophetic.html.

3. Early, "Apostolic Impartation and Prophetic Activation for Destiny."

4. "7203a. roeh," BibleHub.com, accessed December 19, 2015, http://biblehub.com/hebrew/7203a.htm.

5. Christianity.com, "Seer: Easton's Bible Dictionary," accessed April 5, 2016, http://www.christianity.com/bible/ dictionary.php?dic-ebd&id=3258.

6. "8104. shamar," BibleHub.com, accessed December 19, 2015, http://biblehub.com/hebrew/8104.htm.

7. "Bible Verses About Perceive, to," *Forerunner Commentary*, BibleTools.org, accessed December 19, 2015, http://www .bibletools.org/index.cfm/fuseaction/Topical.show/RTD/CGG /ID/9216/Perceive-to.htm.

8. "Strong's #4396: *prophetes*," BibleTools.org, accessed December 19, 2015, http://www.bibletools.org/index.cfm /fuseaction/Lexicon.show/ID/g4396/page/3.

9. "Strong's #5197," BibleTools.org, accessed December 19, 2015, http://www.bibletools.org/index.cfm/fuseaction/Lexicon .show/ID/H5197/nataph.htm.

APPENDIX D
WOMEN AND PROPHECY

1. Stanley M. Horton, "Rediscovering the Prophetic Role of Women," EnrichmentJournal.ag.org, accessed December 19, 2015, http://enrichmentjournal.ag.org/200102/080_prophetic _role.cfm.

CONNECT WITH US!

CHARISMA HOUSE

(Spiritual Growth)

 Facebook.com/CharismaHouse

 @CharismaHouse

Instagram.com/CharismaHouseBooks

SILOAM

(Health)

Pinterest.com/CharismaHouse

REALMS

(Fiction)

Facebook.com/RealmsFiction